Stephen Dykes Bower

Twentieth Century Architects

RIBA ⌗ Publishing

Stephen Dykes Bower

Twentieth Century Architects

Anthony Symondson

© Anthony Symondson 2011

Published by RIBA Publishing, 15 Bonhill Street,
London EC2P 2EA

ISBN 978-1-85946-398-7

Stock Code 74807

British Library Cataloguing-in-Publication Data
A catalogue record for this book is available from the British
Library.

Publisher: Steven Cross
Commissioning Editors: Lucy Harbor and Neil O'Regan
Series Editors: Barnabas Calder, Elain Harwood and Alan
Powers
Production Editor: Susan George
Copy Editor: Ian McDonald
Typeset by Carnegie Book Production
Printed and bound by W.G Baird, Antrim

RIBA Publishing is part of RIBA Enterprises Ltd.

www.ribaenterprises.com

Front cover photo: St John's, Newbury, completed in 1957
© James O. Davies, English Heritage

Back cover photo: Stephen Dykes Bower at Quendon Court,
1980
© Gavin Stamp

Frontispiece: Holy Spirit, Southsea, designed by J. T.
Micklethwaite and Sir Charles Nicholson, restored after
bomb damage and embellished by Stephen Dykes Bower,
1944–58
© Elain Harwood

Foreword

Shortly before Stephen Dykes Bower's 90th birthday in 1993, I asked Anthony Symondson whether he might write a short essay to accompany an illustrated list of works by this architect whose lifetime achievement was still hardly known outside a small circle of his friends. After much delay, and on a much grander scale of text and illustration than initially envisaged, the present book is the result. Nobody else could have written it, informed as it is by Father Symondson's many years of correspondence and conversations with Dykes Bower, his perceptive eye and his unrivalled knowledge of Anglican architecture.

It is particularly appropriate that it should be published in this series, for which the Twentieth Century Society proposes the subjects, since the Society does not discriminate between styles, believing that good work can be found in all the styles current during the period. The arrival of Modern architecture in Britain produced an unbridgeable division on both sides that remains even now. For Dykes Bower, as for his contemporaries who practised in a classical style, such as Raymond Erith, Donald McMorran and Francis Johnson (all of whom have now received admiring tributes in book form), tolerance of Modernism was unthinkable, as the opposite viewpoint was for most of the Modernists themselves. Dykes Bower felt at times that he was the victim of organised bullying and exclusion and Father Symondson's text reminds us of the bitterness arising from these opposing views.

The commitment of Dykes Bower and his few post-war anti-Modernist colleagues was not simply to historic styles, but to the beliefs and practices for which they were a vehicle, including the continuity of historical memory, the beauty of natural materials and the craftsmanship involved in working them, and the possibility that the architect could solve problems in a lasting and inventive way that harmonised with places and made them more beautiful. He was strangely unenthusiastic about his few completely new buildings, among which St John's, Newbury is the grandest, and perhaps felt more comfortable when he had more of a context in which to work.

The field of church work brought additional problems, because Dykes Bower lived through a period in which Modern architecture was coupled to ideas of liturgical reform that tried to model the future on an imagined distant past, represented by austere surfaces and unrefined shapes. The combination was a forceful one, as another book in this series, *Robert Maguire and Keith Murray* by Gerald Adler makes clear, but it was an emotional rather than a logical link that tended to exclude other choices. At

opposite: **St Nicholas', Great Yarmouth, Norfolk, 1953–69, painted organ case designed by Dykes Bower and Hugh Mathews**

the same time Dykes Bower fell foul of the new orthodoxy in architectural conservation that ordained a clear separation between the styles and materials of past and present, and a veneration of ancient building fabric regardless of its practical problems or visual incongruity.

Second only to visiting the buildings, the book, enhanced by the new colour photographs taken by James O. Davies and Steve Cole of English Heritage, is the best way of judging Dykes Bower's ability to make the past come alive in the present, orchestrating space and light to achieve ethereal beauty and calm in which sparkling colour often plays a part. Like the Victorian predecessors he most admired, Dykes Bower understood Gothic as a set of universal design and construction principles without historical limitations.

Three architectural and social trends that have occurred since his death indicate that he might have been a precursor rather than a last ditch survivor of a moribund creed. The first is 'The New Ornamentalism', in which prominent architects have begun to apply repeat patterns to the surfaces of buildings. While the results are not normally intended to resemble traditional buildings, this represents a significant step away from Modernism's long-lasting prohibition of pattern and ornament. Dykes Bower was a master of painted pattern, in succession to the Victorians, and, especially at St John's, Newbury, a master of patterned brick. He saw these enrichments as integral to the character of the whole building.

'New Ornamentalism' has so far created decoration almost entirely through the computer manipulation of 'found' imagery, often at an enlarged scale. Even at Bury St Edmunds, the vault in the crossing was finally cut by computer when the job passed out of the hands of Dykes Bower's successor, even though a cheaper estimate had been given for cutting it by hand with what would undoubtedly have been a better and more lively effect. Dykes Bower used hand drawing in the office, often at full size, and hand making by carving, painting, forging and stitching to create precise but sensitive results impossible with computers. The Modern Movement often showed more appreciation of craftsmanship than has been credited to it, but even so, there was a fatalistic belief that economic pressures would gradually squeeze it out as a normal way of making a living, and this became a self-fulfilling prophecy. Dykes Bower sustained the careers of craftsmen and specialist firms, from the embroidery of Watts & Co to the metalwork of Frank Knight, Norman Furneaux and Eric Stevenson, and the painted decoration of William Butchart and Campbell Smith & Co. In churches, their work was not reserved for a privileged minority, but was available to everyone. It remains to be seen how far a few recent books arguing for the necessity of skilled hand work in a digital age as a preserver of sanity could shift long-held contrary assumptions, but if they do, then Dykes Bower's insistence on nothing but the best quality will be vindicated.

The third area in which Dykes Bower has much to offer the present is in his focus on beauty. Recent writers such as Alain de Botton have revived discussion of this word in relation to architecture, but insisted that the discussion should only concern contemporary Modernism. There seems no justification for restricting such a universal term in this way. As with craftsmanship, in Dykes Bower's words, 'what has been done once can be done again.'

Dykes Bower's method of creating spaces for worship also differs from the orthodoxy of the post-war years in that, like most music, it mostly does not communicate on a literal level with images and symbols, but works in an immersive way on the subconscious of the worshipper. In this sense, it comes close to a form of abstraction.

Implicit in the book is a call for conservation of Dykes Bower's work. The picture of the church of the Holy Spirit, Southsea that forms the frontispiece of this book is now a historical record, only a few years after it was taken. The Church of England, under pressure from many directions and removed by its own planning system from the mainstream of historic building control, can suddenly destroy the beauty accumulated over past centuries, and even The Twentieth Century Society, the only pressure group devoted to preserving the best buildings in all styles of the period, cannot always hold back the tide.

First, knowledge is needed about what was designed by whom, and why. Then judgement needs to be applied, not only in respect of individual aspects of a scheme, but the effect of the whole thing which can as easily be spoilt by the wrong additions as by taking things away. Dykes Bower believed in beauty above all, and while respecting the past, believed that it must be integrated in a coherent architectural vision. If the book succeeds in helping people to understand this vision and pursue it, then it will have served its purpose.

ALAN POWERS

Acknowledgements

I am grateful to Alan Powers for his patience and encouragement in bringing this book to fruition. It would not have achieved its present form without his editorial skill. Next comes Warwick Pethers, with whom I have discussed it and who has proved unfailing in his assistance with providing information. The Gothic Design Practice commissioned Robert Gladden to compile the list of works. Among Stephen Dykes Bower's partners and assistants, I must thank Hugh Mathew and the late Alan Rome for information about Dykes Bower's drawing office and methods of design. I must also thank Professor Gavin Stamp for many conversations and for reading an earlier version of the text. I am grateful to Lorna Scott, archivist to the University of Gloucester; Martin Astell of the Essex Record Office; and the Revd John Hunwicke, formerly of Lancing College, for valuable help. Finally, I have to thank the Very Revd Michael Holman SJ, Provincial of the British Province of the Society of Jesus, for authorising the publication of this book and the Superiors of the Jesuit communities at Stonyhurst College, Lancashire; the Sacred Heart, Wimbledon; and Farm Street Church, Mayfair, for giving me the time to write it. ANS

When this publication was first announced in 1993, funds were generously subscribed by the late Peter Foster, architect; the late Canon Edward Carpenter; the late Michael Gillingham; Donald Findlay; and Merton College, Oxford. For the present publication, additional funds have been generously contributed by The Golden Bottle Trust and the Marc Fitch Fund.

The English Heritage photographers Steve Cole and James O. Davies have contributed nearly all the colour photographs, taken during 2010–11. We are grateful to all the churches and other institutions who have granted access for photography, and in particular to Mark McVay and Hannah Talbot at St Paul's Cathedral. Lucinda Walker at the National Monuments Record; Anne Drewery, Lancing College; Christine Reynolds at Westminster Abbey Library; Edward Bottoms, Architectural Association; and Michael Hall have been very helpful in providing photographs.

A number of churchwardens and incumbents have kindly answered questions, and entries for the list of works have been checked by authors of revised *Pevsner Buildings of England* volumes, James Bettley, Alan Brooks and Michael Bullen.

The editorial team at RIBA Publishing, Matthew Thompson, Susan George, Neil O'Regan and Ian McDonald have helped to bring the project to a long-awaited completion. AP

opposite: Norwich Cathedral organ case

**TWENTIETH
CENTURY
SOCIETY**

*Without the Twentieth Century Society an entire chapter of Britain's recent
history was to have been lost. It was alert when others slept. It is still crucial!*

Simon Jenkins, writer, historian, journalist

The Twentieth Century Society campaigns for the preservation of architecture and
design in Britain from 1914 onwards and is a membership organisation which you are
warmly invited to join and support.

The architecture of the twentieth century has shaped our world and must be part
of our future; it includes bold, controversial, and often experimental buildings that
range from the playful Deco of seaside villas to the Brutalist concrete of London's
Hayward Gallery. The Twentieth Century Society produces many publications of its
own to increase knowledge and understanding of this exciting range of work. The
Twentieth Century Architects series has enabled the Society to extend its reach through
partnership with RIBA Publishing and English Heritage, contributing the contacts and
expertise needed to create enjoyable and accessible introductions to the work of architects who deserve more attention. In the process, the books contribute to the work of
protecting buildings from demolition or disfigurement.

Previous volumes in the series have already had a major impact. Our nomination of
"British Brutalism" to the 2012 World Monuments Watch was successful in part due
to Alan Clawley's *John Madin* focusing on Birmingham's Central Library as this architect's outstanding work. The recent Oxford Dictionary of National Biography has also
followed our lead and included entries on Donald McMorran (of *McMorran & Whitby*)
and Gordon Ryder (of *Ryder & Yates*).

We propose buildings for listing, advise on restoration and help to find new uses for
buildings threatened with demolition. Join the Twentieth Century Society and not only
will you help to protect these modern treasures, you will also gain an unrivalled insight
into the groundbreaking architecture and design that helped to shape the century
though our magazine journal and events programme.

For further details and on line membership details see *www.c20society.org.uk.*

CATHERINE CROFT

DIRECTOR

opposite: American War Memorial Chapel, St Paul's Cathedral

Introduction

Gothic architecture in England has nearly died twice, once at the end of the Middle Ages and again in the twentieth century. Dykes Bower's career is a tale of the second decline of Gothic, following its rebirth in the nineteenth century. Victorian Gothic moved toward Continental models before returning in the 1870s to A. W. N. Pugin's combination of English precedents and a search for beauty involving many craft skills making a unified work of art. The later years of the century represented a peak of creativity, attracting the attention of the German critic Hermann Muthesius, which has sometimes been seen as a stylistic backwater. This suited the high churchmanship of the time, and became the mainstream style well into the new century, reaching the highest standards of perfection.

Church building was never simply a matter of stylistic choice, for the requirements for the celebration of Mass and the Divine Office were the functional spring of Pugin's planning, and as important as his other contributions to the Gothic. The revival of liturgical worship that he initiated in the Roman Catholic Church was echoed by analogous developments in the Church of England. In Anglican churches the centre of interest is constantly shifting between altar and pulpit, but the architects in whose steps Dykes Bower followed were Anglo-Catholics, inspired by the rediscovery of the meaning and value of the sacraments, intent on building churches designed for eucharistic worship. They were convinced that a Catholic expression of the Church of England, centred on the altar, would evolve in the twentieth century.

'Architecture is a traditional art,' as *The Times* art and architecture critic Charles Marriott wrote in 1924 in his book *Modern English Architecture*, 'proceeding by evolution. That is to say, the architecture of any place at any period is not a simple sum in addition of preceding styles and characters, but a consequence of them; the net result of influences which may or may not be apparent in the existing form; and modern English architecture can only be explained with reference to the Greek and Gothic revivals of the nineteenth century.'[1]

Modern Gothic was not narrowly nationalistic or antiquarian, despite an enduring love for England. While building St Cyprian's, Clarence Gate (1901–3), J. N. Comper (1864–1960) defended himself, and the Modern Gothic school, from this reproach by first making an appeal to beauty: 'Beauty is the star which I follow and it has led me into many lands and in each land the light is different and then I worship, and have no desire to confuse one light with another or to put it out by my own artificial flame. But it must be a living light sufficient to see by, no mere antique lamps from which the flame has gone out.' And he made a second appeal to the living application of Gothic in terms

opposite: **St Edmundsbury Cathedral**

of continuity and language: 'By *medieval architecture* I mean the best development of our National English Architecture which is no more and no less medieval than is Shakespeare. Both were developments of the Middle Ages, but both *usher in the modern world*.'[2]

Marriott represented the almost forgotten understanding of architecture before the Modern Movement's call for a complete break with the past had been heard in Britain. Dykes Bower and his predecessors saw no barrier to creativity and functionality in reinterpreting the past. As Dykes Bower wrote in a paper, 'The Importance of Style', it was in the late nineteenth and early twentieth centuries that Gothic in England achieved a second climax, producing such large and contrasting buildings as J. F. Bentley's Westminster Cathedral and Sir Giles Gilbert Scott's Liverpool Cathedral, whose achievement 'lay in the persisting ability to find inspiration in style and handle it with originality.'[3]

Comper and others saw modern Gothic not in terms of revival but as the resumption of arrested development. The Gothic style was used as a language possessing its own grammar and syntax. Dykes Bower wrote that his predecessors 'had the good sense to study thoroughly what they admired, to try to emulate what had been done before. This was a rational and not a negative approach. Far from stifling creativeness it stimulated it and the best exponents of the style acquired sufficient mastery to use it with freedom and spontaneity.'[4]

Gothic and Classical architecture were both included in the vision of beauty proclaimed by Comper, at a time when, foreshadowing the dominance of Modernism, Classical design began to be seen as the answer to all architectural problems. Dykes Bower voiced the same idea, believing that:

> *The ultimate judgement of architecture is always the test of beauty – a word less heard than it used to be, possibly because as an ideal it is less sought after ... The prime need of religious buildings is an unmistakable atmosphere of reverence. The concomitant of that is beauty, which will lift people out of themselves and quicken their response to what a church stands for and has to offer. Architects must be zealous not merely for beauty but for the intellectual content of their work. If irreverence and poor quality are not to give more cause for despondency, the importance of style needs to be reaffirmed. Architecture as one of the fine arts, must above all be literate.*[5]

Apart from Comper, two other architects, Temple Lushington Moore (1856–1920) and Frederick Charles Eden (1864–1944), were especially important for Dykes Bower. He followed Moore in being able to think, plan and build in Gothic without any effort of self-conscious stylism. Dykes Bower succeeded Comper as a furnisher and colourist with an instinctive understanding of where to place furniture and stained glass. He learned from Eden artistry, delicacy of detail, texture and taste. These and a few other like-minded architects embodied the quintessence of the Modern Gothic school: nobility of scale; refinement of execution; powerful structure and aspiration; clarity of planning; beauty of materials and workmanship; fidelity to architectural literacy and tradition; and the design of churches as unified works of art, in which the architect exercised complete artistic control. Dykes Bower's work embodied these qualities; he was the natural successor to what seemed at the beginning of the century an unassailable ascendancy.

Then the situation changed, signalling the second death of Gothic. For decades, Dykes Bower stood completely alone as a worthy successor to the Victorian and Edwardian tradition into the late twentieth century, and it could have been supposed that with his death, the second death of Gothic was inevitable. The story of the completion of St Edmundsbury Cathedral, in the spirit of John Wastell, is compelling evidence to the contrary, and shows the potential for Gothic, however improbably, to live on both as a practical building tradition and as an expression of decorative beauty.

Notes

1   Charles Marriott, *Modern English Architecture*, London, Chapman & Hall, 1924, p.71.

2   Letter from J. N. Comper to Provost Ball of Cumbrae Cathedral, 19 April 1902 and the Revd Leonard Comper, 1 November 1901, Private collection.

3   Stephen Dykes Bower, 'The Importance of Style', lecture given to the Cambridge Ecclesiological Society, Jesus College, 1972.

4   ibid.

5   ibid.

1   Early Life, Education and Practice

Early Life

Stephen Ernest Dykes Bower was born at Elton House, Gloucester, on 18 April 1903, the second of four sons of Ernest Dykes Bower, a general practitioner and ophthalmic surgeon, and his wife, Margaret Dora Constance, the youngest daughter of the Venerable John William Sherringham, Archdeacon of Gloucester. Both sides of the family were notable for medicine, music, academia and the Church, inspired by Anglican piety and motivated by religious, civic and social duty – Dr Dykes Bower became High Sheriff of Gloucester.

The Dykes family were clerical and legal, and formed an Evangelical dynasty in Hull closely associated with William Wilberforce. This link was broken in the early-Victorian period by the adoption of Tractarianism by Dr John Bacchus Dykes, the hymnologist and contributor to *Hymns Ancient and Modern*, and reformer of Anglican chants; and the Revd Thomas Dykes, curate of Hull, who was received into the Roman Catholic Church in 1851 and became a Jesuit.

Stephen was the second of the brothers. Michael and Wilfrid became doctors, and John (later Sir John Dykes Bower) a cathedral organist; all were to remain bachelors. From their parents, all four inherited a powerful interest in music. The family members were profoundly influenced by their regular worship in the cathedral. The brothers absorbed the sense of beauty and the wonder which the two arts, architecture and music, can instil even in a child's mind. The Three Choirs Festival was an eagerly awaited event.

Cathedrals became an absorbing interest for Dykes Bower. His parents gave him a box of mid-Victorian German toy bricks, from which he was able to build Gothic cathedrals that, together with houses, augmented childhood drawings of motor cars, ships and railway engines. He collected penny editions of *Notes on Cathedrals*, and by the age of six could identify every English cathedral, even though he could not pronounce all their names. On school holidays he accompanied his elder brother, Michael, on visits to Worcester and Hereford and the abbeys and churches of the West Country.

In the summers of 1916 and 1917, the Dykes Bower family took the vicarage at Newnham-on-Severn, near the Forest of Dean, designed by the local architect, F. W. Waller (1848–1933), and embodying the better features of the late-Victorian house, which stimulated in Stephen an intense interest in domestic architecture. Waller's complicated arrangement of roof ridges and valleys inspired elaborate juvenile roof plans. Thereafter, Stephen planned houses of his own and sought books on modern domestic buildings. Arthur Eaglefield, the Principal of the Gloucester School of Art (of which Mrs Dykes Bower was a governor), introduced him to books by Edwardian

opposite: All Saints, Hockerill, Hertfordshire, 1935–7

designers, while in Gloucester Public Library he discovered the *Studio Year Book of Decorative Art* with its many photographs of Arts and Crafts houses, among which the work of Edwin Lutyens and M. H. Baillie Scott stood out for him. Dr Dykes Bower encouraged this interest, which reflected his own admiration for the work of Richard Norman Shaw, and from these promptings emerged Dykes Bower's desire to be an architect rather than a musician.

Education

In 1916, Dykes Bower was sent as a day boy to Cheltenham College where his musical interests developed, leading in 1920 to an organ scholarship at Merton College, Oxford. He read for honours in Classical Moderations, later transferring to English Literature. Merton was a historic, intellectually respectable, predominantly middle-class college, prudish and not socially intimidating. Photographs of Dykes Bower at this time show him high minded and serious, with dark waving hair parted in the middle. Music and architecture took up most of his spare time. In 1923, Nigel Playfair produced and directed in Merton Hall Philip Massinger's play, *The Duke of Milan*, a stylish production for which Doris Zinkeisen, Playfair's assistant, designed the programme cover and painted the curtains. The orchestra and music were under the direction of Dykes Bower.

above: **The Dykes Bower brothers. Back, left to right, Wilfrid, Stephen, John; front, Michael**

In 1921, he submitted a design for the college war memorial. H. W. Garrod, a Classics Fellow and Librarian, forwarded it for a professional opinion to J. N. Comper, in order to lift Dykes Bower's spirits. Comper did not recommend it, but felt 'the attraction of a youthful work in a directness and freedom from mannerism which is too often lacking in the productions even of distinguished professionals.'[1] When, in the following term, Dykes Bower was introduced to Comper, the latter encouraged him to take up architecture. He was the first architect Dykes Bower had met; in later life, Comper saw him as a rival.

The beauty of the university enchanted Dykes Bower, including the work of those Victorian architects whose approach was approved of by the conservative taste of the time. He discovered the buildings of G. F. Bodley at the Cowley Fathers' church, George Gilbert Scott Junior at St John's College, C. E. Kempe in Pembroke College Chapel, Temple Moore at Pusey House and Comper in the chapel of St John's Home, Cowley, and in Merton Chapel. He disliked Sir George Gilbert Scott's chapel at Exeter College and had reservations about William Butterfield's aggressive Gothic at Keble, but when his brother John became organist to Truro Cathedral, Dykes Bower fell in love with its architect, J. L. Pearson's, work. Further, he saw almshouses as one of the most satisfying expressions of English architecture and embarked on a serious study of them.

In 1924, Dykes Bower entered the Architectural Association School of Architecture, claiming that he did not learn much in five years although the club-like nature of the institution meant that he was able to meet older practitioners. Architecture was taught

above: Record label for the 1931 AA Pantomime. Music composed by Dykes Bower

according to Beaux Arts principles and methods, and Sir Edwin Lutyens (1869–1944) was still admired by many students. Among Dykes Bower's friends were Hugh Easton, the glass painter; Edward Carter, a future librarian of the Royal Institute of British Architects; and J. M. Richards, the critic and architectural writer. Although later a leading proponent of Modernism, Richards was attracted by Dykes Bower's scholarly and precise Victorian manner even while, like most of his contemporaries, bemused by his enthusiasm for church architecture and the Gothic Revival. Together they toured the cathedrals of Northern France. Some thought Dykes Bower a throwback to the nineteenth century, who should have been at the school 50 years earlier. In 1928, he published a review of Kenneth Clark's *The Gothic Revival: A Study in the History of Taste* in a short-lived student magazine, showing his knowledge of the Gothic Revival and an unprejudiced admiration for the work of Sir George Gilbert Scott, despite his belief that the best work of the revival was accomplished after Scott's death in 1878.[2]

Dykes Bower was popular and threw himself into theatrical life, playing King Henry VIII in *Catherine Parr* and Lady Macbeth in *The Rehearsal*, two plays by Maurice Baring produced in 1927. He started a Madrigal Society, took part in debates and succeeded H. S. Goodhart-Rendel as director of music at the annual pantomime. This led to three triumphs. The first, in 1929, was *The Tale of Silas Bagg*, written by Edward Carter with lyrics by J. M. Richards and music by Dykes Bower. Then, in 1930 and 1931,

above: **The Sailor's Return sketch in the AA Pantomime, 1931**

came two entertainments by R. Y. Gooden: *The Sailor's Return*, set on Yarmouth Quay in 1815 – the part of Ebony was played by Jane Drew – and *The Lass with a Delicate Air*, adapted from *The Happy Hypocrite*, a short story by Max Beerbohm of 1897. Dykes Bower wrote music for both and played it on the piano. He liked the work of George Gershwin and there are echoes of the latter's influence in his surprisingly unstarchy compositions, typical of the dance music of their time.

Richards remembered that there was no support for the new architecture among the wider intelligentsia, whose interest remained 'wholly antiquarian' and who were 'usually patrons of the Georgian Revival'.[3] Although Victorian architecture was out of fashion, its richness and variety and the surviving quantity of its relics interested Dykes Bower and a few discerning contemporaries.

Dykes Bower's contact with F. C. Eden, an undeservedly obscure church architect of the early twentieth century, evolved in the manner of a traditional master and pupil relationship. John Betjeman considered Eden a creative genius, only 'a little lower down the scale' than Comper as one who had 'transformed church architecture in England'.[4]

Eden and Comper, contemporaries in Bodley's office, were aesthetes sharing common architectural and liturgical ideals, intentions, taste and the same Anglo-Catholic churchmanship while enjoying a guarded, if polite, rivalry, founded upon sidelong glances of mutual admiration, pointed private observations and silent borrowing of finishes and styles of workmanship. They used the same wood and stone carvers, embroideresses and colourists. Eden was influenced by Comper's painted glass and embroidery techniques while Comper followed Eden's use of burnished gold and, on occasion, the disposition of rood figures. Comper was the better architect and publicist while Eden abhorred publicity but was the more delicate artist. They passed on their fastidiousness of taste to Dykes Bower.

Dykes Bower admired the chaste, impersonal beauty of Eden's work, its impeccable taste and exquisite feeling for detail, its sensitivity and refinement. They met in 1930, when Dykes Bower was working in Chelsea as an assistant to Kennedy and Nightingale (best known for their extension to the Royal Geographical Society) and joined the Oxford and Cambridge Music Club at No. 6 Bedford Square as a place to live. Eden also lived in the square and their introduction helped Dykes Bower to establish himself in the worst years of the Depression. His first salary was £2 a week, raised to £3 at a second firm, and to £6 when, briefly, he worked for the Great Western Railway's architect's department at Paddington; he described their work as appalling.

When Eden came to see Dykes Bower's susceptibility to beauty he turned the young designer's mind towards church architecture. Despite an age difference of nearly 40 years, they were empathetic and Eden welcomed him to his house, filled with beautiful objects, where he dined by candlelight, reading detective novels and Latin liturgical texts.

From schooldays Eden had regularly travelled on the Continent, and early in his friendship with Dykes Bower he had included him and Guy Lindsey in one of his tours

of Northern Italy, the country that had become his spiritual home. They sketched, measured buildings, looked at pictures, enjoyed good food in modest restaurants, heard Mass in sunlit churches, and searched antiques dealers for church ornaments, old vestments and embroidery, statues and furniture to be brought back for use in English churches. For Dykes Bower it was an education in taste. Eden trained his eye, disciplined his judgement and taught him the architectural principles he had learned from Bodley. Eden also introduced him to church architects of his generation and encouraged Dykes Bower to join the Art Workers Guild and the St Paul's Ecclesiological Society, then the main repository of knowledge and study of Gothic Revival church architecture. He was later elected a Fellow of the Society of Antiquaries.

Practice before 1945

Dykes Bower's first commission was to restore and enlarge the stone-built Beech Cottage at Lower Beeding in Sussex for his uncle, Colonel Sherringham, with proposals which included a sleeping verandah. His later domestic works were confined to a few private houses, estate cottages, vicarages and adapting and reducing country houses to post-war conditions. These were invariably in the Georgian style or in the vernacular tradition, and were as carefully planned and detailed as his churches.

above left: St Germans, Roath, Cardiff, Bodley and Garner, 1881–4, Lady Chapel by F. C. Eden
above right: All Saints, North Cerney, Gloucestershire, alterations and additions by F. C. Eden from 1913

In 1931, Dykes Bower qualified as an Associate of the Royal Institute of British Architects and registered as a private architect, making a mark with book reviews for the *RIBA Journal*. Dykes Bower collaborated with his friend, R. Y. Gooden, on an entry for the headquarters of the Institute. Their severe, rather forbidding, monumental Classical design was considered more harmonious in its setting than Grey Wornum's winning entry.

Dykes Bower's first ecclesiastical works were for Gloucestershire churches: a new high altar for the church at Standish, where his grandfather had been rector, and a chapel for Redmarley D'Abitot.Both were commended in the *Builder*.[5] He designed a new church for Yorkley, in the Forest of Dean, but only the vicarage was built.

The designs were well received by the Bishop of Gloucester and by William Iveson Croome, the Secretary to the Diocesan Advisory Committee and a member of the Central Council for the Care of Churches. Croome was difficult to please, but Eden told him how much he liked Dykes Bower and encouraged him to seek out his work.

Croome was one of the last of a rare breed of late-Victorian and Edwardian country gentlemen who, being men of taste and scholars in their own right, often bachelors, placed their knowledge and energy at the service of the Church. As Squire of North Cerney in Gloucestershire, he spent the 55 years from 1912 restoring and then furnishing the medieval parish church to the designs of Eden and, later, of Dykes Bower. All Saints is one of the most beautiful churches in the Cotswolds, a unified work of art furnished in an eclectic style combining a rare late-medieval stone pulpit and painted glass with later seventeenth- and eighteenth-century furniture and exquisite new work by Eden. This incorporated late-medieval and Renaissance figures, and church ornaments discovered on the Continent by Croome in company with Eden and Walter Tapper.

above left: House at Lower Beeding, West Sussex, 1931
above right: Curate's house, Yorkley, Gloucestershire, 1931

Dykes Bower, whose early patronage was largely organised by family influence and connections, was fortunate to have Croome as an ally and to be given so many opportunities in his native county. Following Truro, in 1933, after a brief interval at New College, Oxford, John Dykes Bower was appointed organist to Durham Cathedral. This led to Stephen being given work in Truro and Durham cathedrals, notably in 1935 when he designed St. Bede's Altar, 3.4 metres (11 feet) long, in the Chapel of the Nine Altars.

This altar was remarkable for its frontal, designed in association with Mary Symonds, one of the most accomplished embroideresses of the early twentieth century and often used by Eden. The colouring was related to the stained glass and stonework, reddish and grey, of the chapel. The dominant note was scarlet with a crimson inclination, according to the fall of the light. Three star-shaped panels were brightly linked together by gold strapwork that enclosed seventeenth-century Spanish roundels of embroidery bought in Florence, floral and foliated in design, which supplied exactly the proportion of green to balance the red. Intermediate panels, also enclosed by gold strapwork, repeat the quatrefoils carved on the wall above, relating both the form and colour of the altar to its surroundings. The powerful altar ornaments, executed by Comyns & Sons, were designed to integrate with the heavy mouldings of the east wall.[6]

After the Second World War his brother, Michael, was practising as a doctor in Exeter. It was through his influence that Dykes Bower was given the work, in succession to Eden, of redesigning the Bishop's Palace there. The best portions were retained as the bishop's quarters but the rest were made into the cathedral library, diocesan offices and vestries.

In 1936, three years after the death of Dr Dykes Bower, the family presented silver ornaments for the new altar of the nave of Gloucester Cathedral in his memory. The altar was designed by Dykes Bower in relationship to the large-scale, rounded Norman piers and great size of the nave, of which it was the focal point and climax. It was covered with a pall of rich purple velvet worked with old Italian embroidery, which he had discovered on his journey with Eden. It had been mended and rearranged by Mary Symonds, and she shaped the pall to hang in folds at the corners and, in order to retain the necessary appearance of austerity, used a heavy roll for the hem instead of a fringe. The altar was illustrated in *The Times* and occasioned a leader describing the growth of improvements to the furniture of English cathedrals.[7]

A new home had to be found for Mrs Dykes Bower, and it was planned that Dykes Bower would share it. She said she did not mind where she lived, stipulating only that nothing would induce her to move to Essex. But Dykes Bower had been shown Quendon Court, near Saffron Walden, on the Essex–Hertfordshire border. Although the five-bay, two-storeyed house of red brick from 1780, with a later projecting Dutch-gabled wing, had been heavily Victorianised in the 1880s, spoilt by ugly bay windows of stone, covered in ivy, provided with no sanitation, water or mains supplies and had been unoccupied for four years, inside it was large, airy and fairly unspoilt. It stood back from the main road through the village and was set in a big wooded garden, of three hectares (seven-and-a-half acres), next to a meadow that linked the house to Quendon Wood.

top: Lychgate, St Nicholas', Standish, Gloucestershire, 1935
above: High Altar, St Nicholas', Standish, Gloucestershire, 1935

Mrs Dykes Bower was persuaded to live there because of its proximity to Hertfordshire. Quendon Court was bought for £1,200, and they moved in with two servants from Gloucester in 1935. During the ensuing years that she lived at Quendon, she came to be charmed by Essex.

The sash windows in plain reveals in the Georgian front elevation were returned to their original form, unattractive small extensions were removed, elegant wrought-iron handrails, painted white, were put up on either side of the pedimented door case, and some cramped spaces inside were eliminated to improve the rooms. House and garden were kept tidy and austere, the latter carefully laid out and divided into walled enclosures with herbaceous borders; and green, shaded spaces were formed by hedges, lawns and shrubs. Oriental and European embroidered textiles, chosen for their perfection, were framed and hung on white walls. The family furniture was meticulously arranged and chandeliers suspended from the ceilings of the principal rooms, which remained largely unchanged for the next 60 years apart from the gradual acquisition of eighteenth-century china and early-Victorian porcelain.

From 1935, Quendon Court served the dual function of home and one-man office. In Quendon, a linear village of 120 inhabitants that remained unspoilt largely through his influence, Dykes Bower restored eighteenth-century cottages, built a few new ones and worked on his neighbours' houses and gardens.

above left: Grave of Ernest Dykes Bower, Standish, 1936
above right: High Altar, St Bartholomew's, Redmarley d'Abitot, Gloucestershire, 1932

The 1930s was a more promising decade for church work than might be supposed. The 20 years between the two world wars formed a period of rapidly progressing housing schemes in all parts of the country, for whose inhabitants the Church of England felt obliged to build new churches.

All Saints, Hockerill, at Bishop's Stortford in Hertfordshire was Dykes Bower's first major commission, designed in 1936, when he was 33, after an earlier church of 1851 by George Pritchett had been destroyed by fire. The committee asked that as much as possible of the remains and materials of the previous church should be used and that the choir should be in the chancel. Beyond that, Dykes Bower had a free hand.

Dykes Bower increasingly came to admire the freshness and refinement of the work of Bodley and George Gilbert Scott Junior and the latter's pupil, Temple Moore, and these influences are apparent at Hockerill. He was also stimulated by Comper's paper, *Further Thoughts on the English Altar, or Practical Considerations on the Planning of a Modern Church*, 1933, reviewing it in the *RIBA Journal* to the author's pleasure. Dykes Bower was one of the few who understood Comper's theories. He absorbed their emphasis on the pre-eminence of religious faith, beauty and unity of design and

above: **The Bede Altar, Durham Cathedral, 1934–5**

workmanship, complete artistic control, and the dependence of architecture upon the Western European tradition augmented by Islamic references.

While All Saints retained the refinement of the school of Bodley in mouldings and detail, the structure, use of materials, freedom from stylistic convention, and finishes reflect the mastery of Moore. In the interior, the furniture shows the influence of Eden and Comper in the assured adoption of the Classical style in a Gothic setting.

The arcades dictated the scale. A simple plan of a nave and two aisles leads to a long chancel, broken at the west end by a structural narthex formed within the base of a saddleback tower. This created a baptistery placed in axial relationship with the high altar. All Saints was admired at the time for its combination of originality with traditional planning. The east wall is pierced by a large rose window with delicate, cusped tracery, filled with painted glass of Christ in Majesty and the Apostles by Hugh Easton, leaving the lower wall free as a background for the high altar. This is raised on shallow steps and contained within Classical pillars, originally intended to carry cherubim, decorated in ivory, gold, red and black, and an especially woven dorsal from Watts & Co. in red and two shades of gold, with a border of deep red velvet. This arrangement is neither a ciborium magnum (or baldacchino), or a Classical version of a Gothic altar with ridel posts – named after the *rideaux*, or curtains, that they support. The high altar had a frontal enriched with panels of old Italian embroidery, completed by

above: **Nave altar, Gloucester Cathedral, 1935–6**

top: Quendon Court

above: Quendon Court from the air, with the Drawing Office (with cupola) to the rear of the house

a red carpet. An unbroken wagon vault of wood and plaster, designed to incorporate concealed lighting into the ceiling, continued from chancel to narthex. The floor is of artificial stone and wood blocks; the furniture of oak.

All Saints is built of stock brick with Kentish ragstone facings, a stone Dykes Bower disliked, ameliorated by the use of wide flush joints instead of raised V-pointing, and as much as possible of the original walls. Stone was used to create a monumental effect in the gently battering walls of the tower, capped by red tiles. This is continued in the battered buttresses, which flank the aisles and make a major contribution to the outline and elevations of the chancel. All Saints is as finished and satisfying, crisp and noble from without as within, and was well publicised.

Although Moore, Comper and Eden influenced All Saints, it is distinctive to Dykes Bower alone and stands apart from the majority of ecclesiastical buildings of the time. It remains his best church and shows what he might have achieved if he had had more opportunities. In design, mastery of planning, detail and control it contains the seeds of St Edmundsbury Cathedral and St John's, Newbury. But he was saddened by later alterations, made without consultation by insensitive incumbents.[8]

above: **All Saints, Hockerill, Hertfordshire, 1935–7**
opposite: **All Saints, Hockerill**

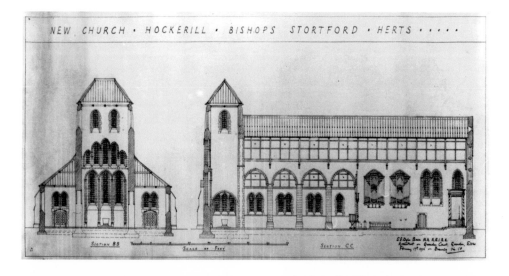

top: All Saints, Hockerill, sections
above: West door; Lady Chapel altar, All Saints, Hockerill

During the period when Hockerill was his main preoccupation, Dykes Bower was given a major restoration of St James's, Wednesbury, in Staffordshire. This Black Country church was a pioneer Anglo-Catholic parish and St James's, a Commissioners' church, had been designed by W. Horton in 1847–8 in the Early English style; enlarged by the addition of a long chancel, designed by Griffin & Weller in 1857; and extended further with an apse in 1865. Dykes Bower transformed the interior by paving the church throughout with black-and-white marble, whitening the walls, hanging the sanctuary with terracotta silk beneath a Classical valance, carpeting the altar steps in carnation gold, and installing a new lighting system. The glazing was renewed, the exterior stonework repaired, the clock and bells overhauled, and a new heating apparatus set up. The result achieved disciplined, uncluttered perfection with the chairs of dark wood arranged in close-set blocks divided by wide aisles, and the rich furniture freed from the untidy encroachments that had muddled the interior. In addition to saving the church from dereliction, Dykes Bower's work embodied the taste and restraint emblematic of the best church furnishing schemes of the period.

In 1934 he had entered the competition for building a new chapel for Cuddesdon College, Oxford, then the most influential theological college in the Church of England, founded in 1853. Eric Graham, the Principal, was a cultivated, moderate Anglo-Catholic, imbued with the spirit of the Caroline Divines and the restraint of the Tractarians, who emphasised the continuity of the Oxford Movement with the Pre-Reformation Church and the history of the Church of England since the Reformation, clung closely to the authorised forms of Anglican worship and interpreted them in the most Catholic sense they were able to bear.

The assessor was Edward Maufe who chose H. S. Goodhart-Rendel's design, but it was not built because of the latter's conversion to Roman Catholicism in 1937. Dykes Bower's entry was a confident, well-detailed exercise in the Early English Gothic style and would have complemented the existing buildings by G. E. Street. His youth and inexperience counted against him but another commission of potential consequence was given later, as a consolation prize.

The Principal of Cuddesdon was also vicar of the parish. All Saints, Cuddesdon, was organised as a model of what a parish church in the country ought to be, and the

top: **Altar frontal, All Saints, Hockerill**

students worshipped there on Sunday and went to Evening Prayer daily. It is a beautiful building, but the long chancel created a problem by making the high altar too remote. In 1940, Graham invited Dykes Bower to design a nave altar to be located within the Romanesque crossing. He designed a Classical chancel screen of wrought iron, painted dull black and gold, and placed the altar before it. The altar stood on a Persian carpet and in 1960 was covered with an embroidered pall of rose-red silk finished with a heavy golden fringe. An eighteenth-century crucifix and candlesticks of brass were put upon it; and from the low vault hung an eighteenth-century candelabrum. Holy Communion could be distributed on three sides of the new sanctuary. It made a lasting impression on the students and, as time passed, many of them became Dykes Bower's patrons. Here, 25 years before nave altars became customary, Dykes Bower showed that they could be accomplished with dignity and taste.

Two other significant influences in Dykes Bower's early career deserve mention. In 1932, he gave a paper to the St Paul's Ecclesiological Society on 'The Problem of Threatened Churches', followed in 1934 by a second on 'Organs and Organ-Cases' published, with fine illustrations, in the *RIBA Journal*, and in 1935 a third on 'Durham Cathedral'.

above: **St James, Wednesbury, interior following reordering by Dykes Bower**

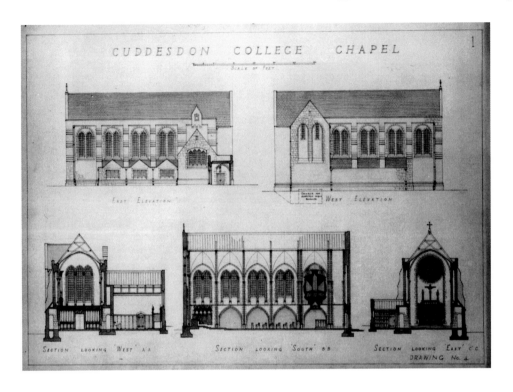

Dykes Bower's interest in organ cases bore fruit in a commission for Norwich Cathedral, where the organ had been dramatically damaged by fire during evensong in 1938. In 1939, he made a design for a new organ case. This was a major commission, given by the learned Dean Cranage, and occasioned a controversy between those who liked unbroken vistas and others who preferred them interrupted by organ screens. Cranage defended the second and wrote in *The Times* that the 'new case will bear comparison with any that has been fashioned in England for at least two centuries. Beautiful in itself, admirably proportioned, and eminently adapted to its position, it will undoubtedly contribute more to the internal loveliness and devotional atmosphere of the Cathedral than the vista, partial or complete'.[9] Standing nobly in a Classical case in the traditional place on the pulpitum, the positive organ faced the choir; the swell was in the middle of the pulpitum, and part of the great and sole tuba faced the nave. Heavy reeds and pedal pipes were out of sight in the triforium, and so spaced that they could speak freely instead of being crowded together or packed into corners. The war intervened to delay its completion, but work was resumed in 1946 and finished in 1950. During construction, Michael Dykes Bower reported to his brother that Dr F. C. Eeles, the Secretary to the Central Council for the Care of Churches, had told him that the

above: Cuddesdon College, Oxford, design for new chapel, 1935

'finest modern organ case he had seen was that at Norwich Cathedral designed by you.'[10]

Dykes Bower's early work was designed alone, without assistants, and demonstrated remarkable powers of maturity and assurance, achieved by rigid self-discipline, hard work and determination. It also showed evidence of an independent mind that was unwilling to be coerced into fashionable compromise. By the time war was declared, he had laid the foundations of an ecclesiastical practice.

At the start of the war, Dykes Bower was conscripted as assistant to the Regional Commissioner at Cambridge, and later to the Ministry of Town and Country Planning. His time was mainly spent on solving traffic problems, which held little interest for him, but he was closely involved in studying the future of Cambridge and came into contact with senior members of the university, including Professor G. M. Trevelyan, the Master of Trinity, and A. B. Ramsey, the Master of Magdalene College and Chairman of the Cambridge Preservation Society, who was impressed by Dykes Bower's conservative approach to the post-war development of the city. His work there led to commissions at Queens', St John's and Magdalene, and to the design of a new church in an outlying suburb.

above left: All Saints, Cuddesdon, Oxford, New Sanctuary at Crossing, 1940
above right: Norwich Cathedral organ model, 1939, made by a sixteen-year-old boy
opposite: Norwich Cathedral organ, 1939–50

Top and above right: St Saviour's Chapel furnishings, Norwich Cathedral
Above: Jesus Chapel furnishings, Norwich Cathedral

Although Dykes Bower was given his major commissions between 1945 and 1960, in later life he considered the aftermath of the war as a period of enormous difficulty and discouragement. He detested the building restrictions, the shortage of materials and the limitations of war-damage compensation. There was also the frustration of re-establishing a private practice at this difficult time, but by dedicating many hours to his work, often with little financial return, he quickly developed the promising first ten years of professional work into a long and productive career.

Notes

1   J. N. Comper to H. W. Garrod, 7 August 1921, Dykes Bower papers. The letter was shown to me by Stephen Dykes Bower when I began work on this book.

2   Stephen Dykes Bower, 'The Gothic Revival: a study in the History of Taste, Kenneth Clark', *No.35*, Autumn 1929, pp.5–12 (reprinted in *Victorian Society Annual*, 1994, pp.57–60).

3   J. M. Richards, 'The Hollow Victory: 1932-72', Annual Discourse RIBA, *RIBA Journal*, May 1972, pp.132–76.

4   Letter from John Betjeman to J. N. Comper, 12 December 1946. Private collection. Stephen Dykes

Bower, Obituary of Eden, *RIBA Journal,* November 1944, p.25; Edward Hagger, 'F C Eden: Building on Tradition', *The Twentieth Century Church, Twentieth Century Architecture* 3, London, 1998, pp.76–84.

5   *Builder*, 27 March 1931, p.563; *Builder*, 24 November 1933, p.818.

6   *The Times*, 22 May 1935, p.10; *Builder*, 7 June 1935, p.1052.

7   *The Times*, 11 June 1936, p.13.

8   *Builder*, 14 January 1938, pp.85–8.

9   *The Times*, 12 February 1940, p.7.

10 Letter from Michael Dykes Bower to Stephen Dykes Bower, 7 October 1942, Dykes Bower papers.

2   St Paul's Cathedral and St Vedast's

St Paul's Cathedral, London

In 1940, 52 years after it had been completed, the high altar and reredos of St Paul's, a controversial design by G. F. Bodley's partner, Thomas Garner, were damaged by a bomb. Only the altar itself had been destroyed; the rest was intact and the whole could easily have been repaired, but Wren scholars complained that the reredos obscured the sweep of the apse and the full length of the quire and conflicted with the continuity and lucidity of Wren's architecture.

Foremost among the critics was W. Godfrey Allen, the Surveyor to the Fabric; the greater part of his professional life had been spent at St Paul's. Garner's reredos was a thorn in his side as much as it had been in his predecessor, Sir Mervyn Macartney's, and the war gave him the opportunity he wanted to take action.

Allen persuaded the Dean and Chapter that rather than repairing Garner's work, an attempt should be made to execute Wren's own intentions for the east end. These could have involved placing the altar in a setting of some magnificence at the end of an uninterrupted full-length vista of the cathedral, unlike the comparatively insignificant communion table actually installed in his time. A note in *Parentalia* (memoirs written by the architect's son) records that the altar Wren envisaged would have stood under a stately ciborium magnum, or baldacchino, 'of four pillars wreathed, of the Richest Greek marbles, supporting a canopy hemispherical, with proper decorations of architecture and sculpture'.[1] Some tentative sketches, and an incomplete model in the trophy room of the cathedral, suggest that he experimented with the design but never evolved a final version.[2]

These details were given to five invited architects in 1948. Dykes Bower's design was chosen and the Royal Fine Art Commission stated that it was favourably impressed by his proposals. The Dean and Chapter authorised Dykes Bower and Allen to prepare plans for the rearrangement of the sanctuary and an American Memorial Chapel in the apse. Dykes Bower was one of the few admirers of the Garner reredos, but the decision to supersede it was the Dean and Chapter's, as recommended by their Surveyor. A pledge was given (only partly honoured) that the undamaged parts would be taken down and preserved. To this day, fragments are heaped in St Paul's Churchyard; the marble crucifix and an image of the Virgin and Child were for some years incorporated in new chapels but later were removed; the rest vanished.

Allen was responsible for establishing that the baldacchino should stand centrally under the coffered arch that separated the easternmost bay of the quire. It should be oblong rather than square on plan, to conform to the proportions of the bay. It should

opposite: **The High Altar at St Paul's with the American War Memorial Chapel behind**

incorporate the main attributes of Wren's ideal: the wreathed columns, the canopy and the rich decoration and sculpture combined with the essential elements of the religious symbolism of Garner's reredos – the crucified Christ on the altar cross and the risen Saviour, with adoring angels below, on the apex. The material would be oak, toned down to harmonise with the stalls and organ case, richly embellished with gilding and, in places, other colours such as ivory and scarlet. The altar ornaments would be gilt.

Further, the sanctuary levels would be simplified to give room for ceremonial, and Jean Tijou's magnificent wrought-iron screens and the great, early sixteenth-century standard candlesticks by Benedetto da Rovezzano would flank the altar. A new floor, chiefly of black-and-white marble but with some richer marbles in the sanctuary, would

above: **Reginald Kirby's drawing of the High Altar at St Paul's**

be laid throughout the full length of the quire. Stone would be substituted for what remained of Garner's white-and-green marble on the main pilasters of the sanctuary arcade. Finally, the treatment of the stained glass in the two tiers of windows in the apse would form an integral part of the scheme and complete its colour enrichment. Allen's involvement was limited to this specification, although Dykes Bower insisted that he should be recognised as a partner because he was the Surveyor.[3]

Dykes Bower's design was hung in 1949 in the Architecture Room at the Summer Exhibition of the Royal Academy, drawn in colour by Reginald Kirby, his first assistant. It was described by G. Maxwell Aylwin in the *Builder* as 'one that stands out like a jewel from the well-composed wall, and it is, perhaps, its own convincing argument for the treatment which has caused so much stir.' Aylwin believed that it was the only way to emphasise the liturgical climax of the cathedral without defacing Wren's architecture.[4]

Post-war conditions were appalling for executing such a scheme. The work was elaborate and intricate, every detail had to be carefully drawn up real size. Dykes Bower had to marshal woodcarvers, stonemasons, gilders, silversmiths, blacksmiths, ironsmiths, turners and a glass painter. He succeeded by using long-established firms, many of whom traced their origins to the nineteenth century. A few of the workmen were experienced and had not fought in the war; but others were newly demobilised and apprentices who learned their trade working on the baldacchino, and who in many cases continued working for Dykes Bower for the rest of their lives.

The altar is of marble, divided into panels decorated in gilded relief. At each corner, the baldacchino is supported on square piers of white marble, flanked by fluted Corinthian columns decorated with gilded bay wreaths. Above the segmental arches on the east and west sides are wooden valances, enriched with gilded cherubs' heads, tassels and swags of fruit and flowers. At the four corners are large urns carved in wood, two of which were originally in the chapel of Eton College. The drum of the dome is pierced by lunettes divided by winged cherubs' heads. Standing above are four adoring angels, life-size and solidly gilded, grouped round a figure of the risen Saviour. The tall altar cross and candlesticks are of silver gilt and were given by the Goldsmiths' Company.

The workmanship was organised on a collaborative basis. Contracts for the woodwork were placed with Rattee & Kett Ltd of Cambridge, the execution directed by W. F. Haslop, head of the carving department. J. Whitehead & Sons Ltd was responsible for the marble work. The figures of Christ and the angels and the capitals of the columns were carved in the workshops of E. J. & A. T. Bradford Ltd of Borough Road, Southwark, from models made up of laminations of lime, bonded with adhesive.

Each of the four spiral columns consisted of many segments of oak, bonded into the form of an octahedron (a solid formed by eight faces) four-and-a-half metres (15 feet) long, the shaft length of the column. Rattee & Kett executed them, but the columns required to be turned and were taken to the workshops of George Stow & Co. Ltd,

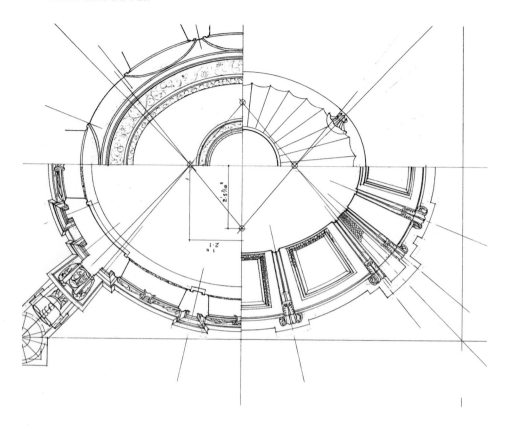

waterworks engineers, of Slough, one of the few firms in southern England to have a suitable lathe for turning pillars of this size. Each column was turned to a smooth, cylindrical shape, into which the spiral groove was then cut, and finished with an entasis. The wreaths were traced onto the column and cut by a woodcarver to leave the pattern in relief. The altar cross and candlesticks were made by Frank Knight, of Wellingborough, a silversmith trained by Comper.[5]

The baldacchino was erected as a memorial from the people of Britain to the men and women of the Commonwealth and Empire who gave their lives in the two world wars. The chapel behind the high altar was a memorial to the dead of the American allies, and Dykes Bower also designed this. The lower walls of the apse were lined with a reredos and panelled stalls of oak, sumptuously carved and gilded. The altar rails of wrought iron were of such distinction that the Victoria and Albert Museum requested copies of the drawings. At the outer ends of the stalls are gilded medallions, set in arabesques, carved in shallow relief with portraits in profile of Allen and Dykes Bower, the Queen and General Eisenhower.

above: **Plan of baldacchino at different levels**

top: Carver working on the baldacchino columns
above left: Carving the figures for the baldacchino
above right: A young workman at Rattee and Kett

The stained glass was designed by Brian Thomas, a fellow member of the Art Workers Guild, and executed by the Whitefriars Stained Glass Studio. Thomas practised as a mural painter before turning to stained glass, which he designed but did not execute. The windows are the dominating feature of the chapel and the one in the centre is the east window of the cathedral. The subjects represent the service, sacrifice and resurrection of the Christian soldier embodied in scenes from the life of Christ.

Dykes Bower made watercolour sketches for each window to guide the artist, defining the pattern and scale but leaving the groups and shields blank. Thomas's windows are exquisite in form and execution, and work successfully as part of a unified whole. Their mellow colour is produced by double flashing and acid etching, which creates patterns without the need for leaded divisions. In the uncoloured parts of the windows, Thomas produced a black-and-white effect, which corresponded to the vibrant contrast of the white Portland stone and soot (so admired by Lutyens) that characterised St Paul's before it was cleaned, and the black-and-white marble of the floor.

The east end of St Paul's took ten years to complete. In 1958 the Bishop of London, in the presence of the Queen and the Duke of Edinburgh, consecrated the altar with chrism. The Queen gave a fair linen cloth. The dean preached the sermon and the Archbishop of Canterbury gave the blessing. The canons wore Edwardian copes stiff

above: **The American War Memorial Chapel, 1958–9**

with embroidery. Dykes Bower's brother, John, directed the music. Trumpeters sounded the Last Post and Reveille. The choir sang 'Now Thank We All Our God'. The steps to the west door were lined with cadets and junior officers from Commonwealth countries training in Britain. As the Queen and the Duke and members of the Royal Family left, preceded by the Lord Mayor bearing the Pearl Sword, the bells pealed out. For London, at least, it was the last of the major demonstrations of royal, civic and military pageantry to commemorate the war.[6]

The high altar, baldacchino and American Memorial Chapel stand alone in Britain as an expression of ecclesiastical design and workmanship of the most finished standard. They equal the earlier work of Grinling Gibbons and Tijou. Nikolaus Pevsner acknowledged that 'the baldacchino makes a fine effect, in keeping with the Baroque qualities of Wren's building.'[7] The ensemble was lent a Continental lustre by hanging in the sanctuary eighteenth-century chandeliers from Gosford Hall in Essex. Some were shocked that the statement was cosmopolitan rather than insular. In Continental Europe, the east end of St Paul's Cathedral was equalled only by the post-war restorations of the Bavarian Baroque churches.

above left: Dykes Bower's portrait on the stalls of the American War Memorial Chapel
above right: Panelling in the American War Memorial Chapel, St Paul's Cathedral

St Vedast's, Foster Lane, London

Restoration gave Dykes Bower some of his best opportunities, first among them the rebuilding of St Vedast's, Foster Lane, one of the 17 churches designed by Sir Christopher Wren that had been destroyed or seriously damaged during intensive German bombing on the night of 29–30 December 1941. Work started in 1953 and in a letter published in the following year Dykes Bower set out his principles for a restoration scheme, siding with H. S. Goodhart-Rendel and John Summerson who felt that reconstruction should be in the spirit of the original but not necessarily literal. The same approach was shared by the cultivated rector Canon C. B. Mortlock. Dykes Bower could not have wished for a more sympathetic patron, and it is partly owing to the good relations they enjoyed and their common assumptions that the restoration was brought to a successful conclusion.

The spire and masonry of St Vedast's had survived relatively unharmed; it was the timber elements, the roofs and the interior furniture and stained glass that were lost. Dykes Bower followed Godfrey Allen's proposal for St Bride's, Fleet Street, that the seating plan should be collegiate, in the form of stalls facing each other, enclosed in the nave within Classical oak screens. In adopting this plan at St Vedast's with only one arcade, Dykes Bower brought into unity random elements that otherwise might have appeared disparate. These were in the form of items of church furniture that he had rescued from dispersal throughout the Diocese of London between 1831 and 1904, during which time 17 Wren churches were demolished.

The octagonal pulpit, with a rich design of fruit and flowers, lions and skulls, is from All Hallows, Bread Street (demolished 1878); the font and cover are from St Anne and St Agnes; the altar is from St Matthew's, Friday Street; the reredos and communion rails from St Christopher-le-Stocks (demolished 1781); and the organ is from St Bartholomew-by-the-Exchange. Dykes Bower achieved 'appropriateness' through rediscovering this furniture and unifying new stalls and panelling by dark-staining the timber – a characteristic of Wren's interiors that few other architects attempted to emulate. Elsewhere, an un-historic, Morrisian treatment of plain oak was preferred, which has now assumed an unpleasant ginger tone. The organ case, pulpit, font and reredos gave the interior of St Vedast's an architectural and visual coherence that is lacking in most other City church restorations.

'The success of St Vedast's', believes Andrew Derrick, 'owes much to the decision of the architect to rely on good-quality fittings, old and new, stained in the traditional manner, with no attempt to pay lip-service to contemporaneity.'[8] The only note with which he quarrels is the use of silver lead, rather than gold, in the plasterwork. This was partly done as an economy, but Dykes Bower defended it as a foil to the wide expanse of the pavement of black-and-white marble. A further note of authenticity was given in the stained glass, by Brian Thomas, of the east windows, which have the same double flashing and acid etching as the windows in St Paul's and produce the same mellow, seventeenth-century colouring that also provides an additional foil to the dark woodwork.

above right: St Vedast's, Foster Lane, the restored interior with glass by Brian Thomas

Dykes Bower designed a new rectory on the site of the Fountain Inn next door to St
Vedast's. To the north of the church was a courtyard, probably the site of a graveyard, a
small seventeenth-century enclave left desolate after the bombing but restored and even
improved upon by Dykes Bower. The house was designed to look onto the courtyard,
and its elevation to Foster Lane was intentionally subservient to the adjoining west front
of the church. Mark Girouard described it in *Country Life* as 'a very enjoyable piece of
Classical design, carried out (with great feeling for the materials used) in brown and
red brick with some stone dressings, and more reminiscent of French and German
Neo-classical work of the early 19th century than of any English prototype.'[9]

The restored cloister and gallery, the re-roofed hall with a new cupola and, above
a continuation of the cloister, the long drawing room windows and delicate ironwork
of the rectory itself, all look onto the paved and cobbled court. It has a central bed
planted with shrubs and a fountain in memory of the vanished Fountain Inn. 'It is',
Girouard thought, 'a secret and peaceful place and a welcome surprise in the rather arid
surroundings of that part of the City.' The plan is ingenious, leading to a top-floor study
and terrace. 'At a time when those who practise in the traditional styles all too often fail
to bring credit to their profession', Girouard found this a shining exception.[10]

top: **The courtyard of St Vedast's**
above: **Elevation of the Rectory, St Vedast's**

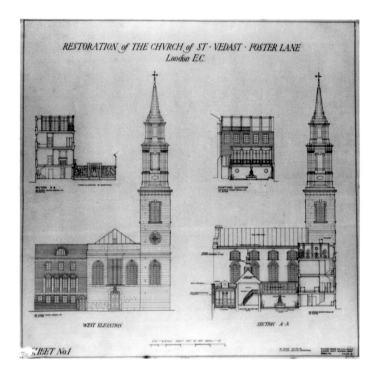

Notes

1 Christopher Wren, Jr, *Parentalia or Memoirs of the Family of the Wrens*, London, T. Osborn and R. Dodsley, 1750, p.282.

2 *The Times*, 1 June 1948, p.10; *Architect and Building News*, 11 June 1948, pp.514–5.

3 *The Times, op. cit.*

4 *Builder*, 6 May 1949, p.553; *Architects' Journal*, 8 December 1949, p.640.

5 *Builder*, 2 December 1949, pp.723–6.

6 *Sphere,* 17 May 1958, pp.243–4, 6 December 1958, pp.378–9; *Illustrated London News*, 6 December 1958 (233), pp.982, 996–7; Alan J. Bune, *New High Altar Canopy of St Paul's: An Account of its Design and Construction*, pamphlet, n.d.; Anon, *The Windows of the American Memorial Chapel, St Paul's Cathedral, London: A descriptive note*, Whitefriars Studio, n.d.

7 Nicholas Pevsner, *The Buildings of England: London Volume One,* Harmondsworth, Penguin Books, 1973, p.138.

8 Andrew Derrick 'Post-war Reconstruction of Wren's City Churches', *AA Files* 26, 1993, pp.27–33.

9 *Country Life*, 2 June 1960, pp.1254–5.

10 ibid.

above left: **St Vedast's, sections and elevations**

3 Westminster Abbey

Dykes Bower was appointed Surveyor to the Fabric of Westminster Abbey in 1951 on the recommendation of Lawrence Tanner, Keeper of the Muniments. At 48, he was the youngest person to hold that office in the twentieth century. His 22 years in the position have been overshadowed by controversies, so that the exceptional nature of what he achieved has never been fully recognised. No Surveyor other than Sir George Gilbert Scott did more to unveil the architectural qualities and beautify the abbey's interior, and what we see today is very largely what Dykes Bower left. This was, of course, only part of an extremely complicated whole, for a great deal of his work was structural, invisible and confined to maintenance.

This work was surrounded by hearsay and rumour. John Summerson said he 'would rather like to go through the archives of DB's period of office and see if a real person – saint or villain – emerges.'[1] Dykes Bower's audit reports, submitted annually to the Dean and Chapter, disclose no villain but an experienced architect, of scholarship, knowledge and educated taste – one who was an artist, who held in veneration the building he was looking after and who recognised its place in the northern European tradition of architecture.[2]

In 1951, the tone of the whole interior was brown; this was not the natural colour of the stone and marble but a discoloration of dust and dirt, aggravated by Scott's application to the stonework of a varnish of shellac. Sir Charles Peers had made a tentative start on cleaning the white surfaces but they appeared so startling that Dean Foxley Norris had them toned to what he described as a 'coffee' colour by the application of wax. The dun colour of the abbey had admirers, including J. N. Comper and George Gilbert Scott Junior, who saw beauty in it, but Dykes Bower found the overall effect repulsive.

As at St Paul's, the work was beset by shortage of materials, the restrictions of war-damage compensation and the difficulty of finding experienced builders and workmen, compounded by the magnitude of what had to be done. The backlog of work since 1939 was so serious that further delay would have imperilled the building. Publicity in the national press emphasised the need for action and Sir Winston Churchill, the Prime Minister, launched an appeal for one million pounds. The Coronation of Queen Elizabeth II in 1953 opened a fund of good will towards the abbey and its plight, and guaranteed the appeal's success.

None of Dykes Bower's plans could have been achieved without the assent of the deans, Alan Campbell Don (dean 1946–59) and Eric Symes Abbott (dean 1959–74),

opposite: **Westminster Abbey looking east, showing the cleaned stonework, lighting and decorated pulpitum**

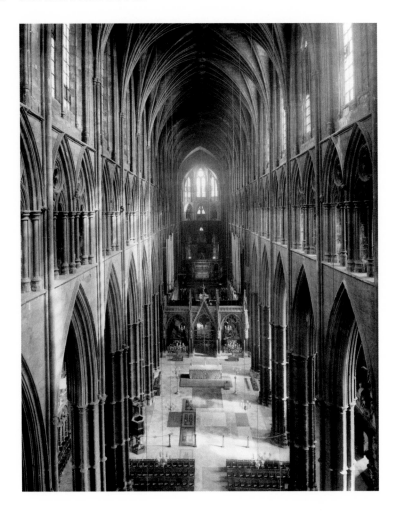

both warmly disposed towards him and sympathetic towards his intentions. The abbey is visited by millions of people; Dykes Bower wanted to make it representative of the standards of the Church of England. By 1973, these standards had shifted beyond recognition but owing to Dean Abbott and Dykes Bower the abbey remained impervious to change.

Dykes Bower's first objective was to return the abbey to its architectural integrity, as close as possible to the mind of Henry of Reyns, King Henry III's mason, but the furniture and monuments reflected the entire development of English history and art. It was a national shrine where much of the work was of paramount significance. By restoration, he did not mean returning the building to a lost period of perfection but letting it speak for itself and allowing the contents to make their own statement.

above: Westminster Abbey before cleaning, and before the installation of Lethaby's lighting fittings, c1911

The three main tasks were cleaning the interior, repairing the roofs and restoring the stonework. Within this framework, Dykes Bower dealt with glazing, lighting, furniture and decoration, designed much new work and gave the interior an appearance that had never before been seen, introducing colour as a unifying element for the first time since the Middle Ages.

At the end of the war the abbey was not only brown, it was in a muddle; there was dirt everywhere. A bomb had brought down T. H. Wyatt's plaster vault in the crossing, executed by Francis Bernasconi in 1803. Many of the windows were damaged and boarded up, too mutilated to be retained. Much broken glass and furniture had been removed to the triforium. Valuable stained glass (notably Comper's noble series of abbots and kings, executed from 1909 onwards, in the north aisle) had been removed for safety and required reinstatement.

Dykes Bower had a better eye for Victorian glass than his contemporaries and admired one damaged window in particular, an unfashionable work of Burlison & Grylls, composed of small figures of kings and queens, archbishops and notable people

above: **The contrast between stonework before and after cleaning**

of the time of King Edward VII, having almost the appearance of medieval glass. James Hora had given the window in 1903 and the scheme of subjects was prepared by M. R. James, the Provost of Eton. To Dykes Bower's regret, the Dean and Chapter declined to reinstate it above Chaucer's tomb in the east side of the south transept, but he used what remained as a glass quarry and set subjects in many places in the abbey, notably King Henry V's Chantry and the Langham Room in Cheyney Gates, the former abbot's house. Medallions from other works were set in grisaille in the windows of the lantern, broken fragments filled the heads of some of the windows in the cloister and a great deal of heraldry was redeployed. Slightly damaged windows were reinstated.

However, it was in its clear glazing that the abbey most benefited. Dykes Bower admired Wren's employment of rectangular rather than diamond quarries, believing that their small size enhanced the architecture and greatly magnified the scale. He judged that 'no medieval church of the first rank can show clear glazing so completely successful.' It was essential to avoid arbitrary contrasts that upset aesthetic equilibrium. In 1953, clear glass was substituted in the triforium for damaged nineteenth-century windows of dark tone. For the first time in almost 100 years an even balance of light was achieved throughout the nave, transepts and apse. 'Through these great clerestory windows there now pours in a radiant flood of light, and the old glass in the three apse windows gains by being the only stained glass at this level.'

Little new glass was put into the abbey in Dykes Bower's time. John S. Bucknall erected Comper's last window, in memory of Sir Henry Royce, posthumously in 1962. Brian Thomas designed the lancets of the north transept in 1957, complementing Sir James Thornhill's rose window, executed by Joshua Price in 1722. In 1946–9, Hugh Easton designed the windows in the King Henry VII Chapel, commemorating the Battle of Britain, for Sir Charles Peers as part of Sir Albert Richardson's scheme of silver-gilt furnishing of the chapel behind the royal tomb. Comper unsuccessfully tried to persuade Sir Kenneth Clark, the Director of the National Gallery, to use his influence to have them removed. These were followed in 1948 by over-scaled figures by Easton, set in white glass, of the Virgin and Child in Abbot Islip's Chantry and of St Michael in St Benedict's Chapel. These lacked force in colour or design, while still drawing attention by their incongruity.

William Iveson Croome reported Dykes Bower's views on glass in a letter to F. C. Eeles:

> He says, rightly, that the best windows are not at first noticed at all, they are just there and so right that they blend into a general fine view, and are part of it. But to do so it is vital that in scale and composition, as well as colour, they should be in harmony with their surrounding features, and as a rule subordinate to them, not clamant by themselves …
>
> He thinks things so bad, and the absence of anybody working on really sound lines so marked, that we ought seriously to consider taking up patterned glass again; an improved form of what was done in the earlier 19th century: i.e. just jewelled borders and the quarries lightly powdered with golden

devices. He thinks this would be (a) safe in most places, (b) quite effective, (c) fairly cheap, and (d) capable of something like mass production; and that its extensive use would save us many headaches and many mistakes.[3]

This interest in patterned glass explains Dykes Bower's work in the lantern of the abbey, the grisaille glazing in St John's, Newbury, and the care he took with stained glass at Bury St Edmunds, Lancing College Chapel and elsewhere. Everything he designed was architecturally conceived.

The internal cleaning of the abbey was started in 1954 and planned for completion to coordinate with the celebration in 1965–6 of the 900th anniversary of the abbey's foundation by St Edward the Confessor on 28 December 1065. Towards the close of 1961, it became possible for the first time to see the high vault as it was when newly built. It seemed miraculous that stone which had become so dark should, after 600 years, regain its original colour by the cleaning properties of nothing but water.

The white light of electricity, first introduced by W. R. Lethaby, was a poor substitute for candles. Even so, Dykes Bower preferred the direct simplicity of Lethaby's handsome

and easily maintained pendant fittings to the 'dramatic subtleties of concealed lighting'. As he wrote, 'The same pattern is used consistently throughout the nave, quire and transepts, and seen in line, it has a stateliness that is appropriate to the Abbey and certainly contrasts favourably with the poor design of comparable fittings elsewhere.' What chiefly marred the appearance of these pendants was the condition of the brass; it was tarnished, black and pitted with old lacquer, although after the coronation in 1953 he was able to have them cleaned.

By the 1960s, the low light level cast by Lethaby's pendants seemed anachronistic, but Dykes Bower detested over-lit churches and theatrical lighting schemes as inimical to architecture. A sub-committee was formed to consider relighting the abbey and invited two firms, General Electric and Troughton & Young, to make proposals for general illumination and demonstrate them in the building, neither of which was satisfactory aesthetically or functionally.

In 1960, following the wedding of Princess Margaret, the Guinness family offered chandeliers for lighting the nave and transepts to commemorate the nonocentenary year. They were to be designed by Miroslav Havel and made by the Waterford Glass Works – a dramatic proposal that took Dykes Bower by surprise, not least because the designs had already been made. He rarely welcomed independent suggestions, so the offer put him in a quandary. The Dean and Chapter had no intention of refusing the gift, while his liking for chandeliers disposed him towards acceptance and he resolved

above: Altar frontal worked by Winifrid Peppiatt at Watts & Co, presented by HM The Queen, 1956

to hang them in the same positions as Lethaby's pendants, but doubled in the transepts, providing illumination of the lower half of the building, complementing the Troughton and Young scheme that had been selected.

Despite his reservations about Havel's design, Dykes Bower eventually agreed that the chandeliers would be 'worthy ornaments, beautiful by day as well as by night.' In the summer of 1963 he travelled to Waterford to settle difficult points. The original design had to be modified, owing to cost, by reduction to two chandeliers to every pair of bays, instead of to each bay. Because the original model would not accommodate enough lamps to light an area twice as big as intended, the size of the chandeliers had to be increased, and he took the opportunity of making other alterations to the design, with the aim of improving the profile and eliminating crudities of detail. Havel and the Waterford Glass Works' design department were not pleased by these interventions but the donors accepted the modifications and the chandeliers were put on public show in July 1965 with the indirect light.

It is a custom that after a coronation the sovereign presents a gift to the abbey, and for Queen Elizabeth Dykes Bower designed a frontal of especially woven blue silk Gothic damask, elaborately embroidered. He wanted to include an upper frontal to conceal the Salviati mosaic behind the high altar, but it was never achieved. The work, completed in 1956, was executed by Watts & Co., a firm of church furnishers founded in 1874 by G. F. Bodley, Thomas Garner and the younger George Gilbert Scott to execute their own designs for textiles and embroidery. Watts had a long association with the abbey, having made the pall for the shrine of St Edward the Confessor and the richly embroidered copes of red velvet designed by J. T. Micklethwaite for the Coronation of King Edward VII in 1903. At All Saints, Hockerill, Dykes Bower had used some of their magnificent figured tapestry for the frontals and dorsals; their patterns were architecturally designed to read from a distance and continuously remained in use.

Watts's work was of a high standard but in Winifrid Peppiatt, who worked the frontal, they had an embroideress of consummate ability, tutored as a young woman at the School of Embroidery of the Sisters of Bethany, run by an Anglican religious order in Clerkenwell, the best workshop of the time, and trained by Comper. Shortly before the war, Miss Peppiatt became a Catholic and had to leave the school, and when Comper subsequently rediscovered her at Watts he exclaimed with delight 'So *this* is where you are!'[4] Dykes Bower reserved his best work for Watts and Miss Peppiatt, and in addition, they looked after much routine work in the abbey under the direction of Canon Hildyard.

In 1964, with the 900th anniversary in mind, Dykes Bower gave Watts a commission for a set of five copes of sumptuous white-and-gold figured silk, especially woven in Lyons on reconstructed seventeenth-century looms. Miss Peppiatt embroidered the hoods, representing a formalised rose in a sunburst, on rose-red French silk. Nothing so magnificent had been presented to the abbey since Micklethwaite's copes and Comper's coronation frontal for King George VI. The other work of similar splendour executed

above: The monument to Lord Hunsdon, after painting

by her for the abbey was a richly embroidered pall of especially woven red Gothic silk damask, designed by Thomas Garner, for the nave altar. It was finished in 1968 and formed the conclusion of Dykes Bower's rich decoration and furnishing of the nave sanctuary.

Had Dykes Bower not given Watts & Co. encouragement and work in the abbey, and in many of the other cathedrals and churches he looked after, the continuity of their original spirit might have been broken and the firm might have foundered.

Dykes Bower's work in furniture and decoration fell into three categories: repair, reinstatement and decoration of existing work, and new design, although he was anxious to look at the abbey as a whole, including the monuments. The majority of these had been neglected or suffered injury over time, and all were as dusty as the rest of the abbey. Above all, Dykes Bower loved the late-Tudor and early-Stuart Artisan Mannerist tombs found in the aisles of the King Henry VII Chapel and filling the chapels radiating from the ambulatory. Nowhere else in the country is there a collection of tombs of the period 1558–1625 of such high order. He saw that they could be one of the distinctive glories of the abbey, and they engaged his interest from the beginning of his surveyorship.

In 1953, the cleaning of St Paul's Chapel disclosed the woeful condition of the tombs, including monuments by Nicholas Stone and Hubert Le Sueur. The colouring and marbles had suffered from corrosive acids in the atmosphere, owing to the failure to keep them polished, and from extensive damage resulting in the mutilation or loss of portions of their design. Dykes Bower had to decide whether it would be desirable to restore original colouring where it could be clearly recognised before time obliterated all trace of it, and how far the damage should be made good. The same problems were discovered in the Chapel of St John the Baptist and it was here that, in the following year, he made his first experiments.

All the monuments, with the exception of the early sixteenth-century tombs of Abbot Fascet and Bishop Ruthall, were cleaned and their heraldry repainted. By far the largest monument in the chapel, and the tallest in the abbey, is Lord Hunsdon's of 1596, which was chosen for its dramatic force to became the exemplar of what monuments of the same period should be: the marble repolished, the ornament gilded and coloured.The big square tomb chest in the centre of the chapel to Thomas Cecil, Earl of Exeter (1523) was in an even greater state of neglect, with many features of its architectural design loose or missing. These were made good, but no attempt was made to restore the lost parts of the sculpture, such as the hands of the two recumbent effigies.

At the same time the tomb of Queen Elizabeth I, by Maximilian Colt (1606), in the north aisle of the King Henry VII Chapel was also partly cleaned and polished; but so many parts of the design were missing and in need of proper restoration and painting that the cleaners were transferred to the two early eighteenth-century Halifax monuments (1715) close by. In this way, a varied selection of tombs of different periods and types was chosen to show how they would respond to treatment. The results

were so pleasing that the experiment was deemed a success, and so began a comprehensive restoration of the abbey tombs. Yet some were startled by the brightness of this achievement and thought the result garish. Dykes Bower reminded them that newness wears off, and at the present time the monuments have achieved a mellow harmony that entirely justifies his decision.

Dykes Bower's methods may seem surprising since current principles of conservation actively discourage, and sometimes legally prohibit, reinstatement of lost features and recolouring. Dykes Bower's principle of restoration was thus: the realisation of the original designer's intention must normally be preferable to perpetual mutilation. But what of the maturing effects of time? Apply that, he said, to a mouth full of bad teeth.[5]

The experiments on Queen Elizabeth's tomb attracted much public interest. Dykes Bower and Dean Don received many letters asking for a complete restoration, but the work was beyond the resources of the abbey's staff. The tomb's splendour depended upon decoration, but this could not be renewed until the large number of missing features in marble and alabaster, vital to the design, had been supplied. Even after the

above: **William Butchart working in Westminster Abbey**

initial cleaning, the full effect was ruined because some were lost: the Queen's effigy lacked its crown, collar and sceptre; the heraldic emblem, a crowned lion, surmounting the south side, should balance a thistle on the north; and several coronets over royal and ducal arms were missing. There was an abundance of evidence in old prints, as well as knowledge of heraldry, to help remedy these defects.

At this point William Butchart, one of the most finished decorators of his generation, was brought in. Dykes Bower recognised that he possessed unique skill and artistry, having been trained by H. A. Bernard Smith, a fellow-pupil of Comper and F. C. Eden at Bodley and Garner's. Smith never practised as an architect but instead established an atelier at 5 Staples Inn, Holborn, where he executed church decoration, assembling an accomplished staff of painters, who were trained by Comper to execute work of the highest order.

Butchart's first job for Comper was in 1930, when he gilded the metal cornice and dolphins which formed the brattishing of the Spanish style screens, or *rejas*, of black wrought iron in the Warrior's Chapel in the abbey. His next major task was the gilding and painting of Bodley's triptych at All Saints, Carshalton, Surrey, in 1932. It was in these works that, for the first time, Comper used water gilding burnished with an agate – a much brighter effect than oil gilding. Comper said that he had never had work done so well; it made him wish he had had his life all over again as he would have employed it in his early work. From that time on, Butchart executed all Comper's painted decoration and gilding. When Smith retired in 1934, following the completion of the decoration of the rood and altar screen at Wymondham Abbey, Norfolk, Butchart set up independently in a small workshop built at the end of his garden in South Croydon.[6]

Hitherto, the monuments had been seen in aesthetic, historical or personal terms but, as Dykes Bower wrote, 'none should be given greater weight than the architectural, which has received the least regard in the past.' After Comper died in 1960, Butchart, by now elderly and in frail health, worked solely at the abbey.

Dykes Bower learned much from his visit to Comper's masterpiece, St Mary's Wellingborough, Northamptonshire (1904–31) soon after its completion, seeing how the pale gold, clear blue, rose-red and emerald green of the painted furnishings and textiles, as clean and pure as the Mediterranean sky, sea and lemon groves, are taken from the tonalities of the Palermitan mosaics in Sicily. These combinations showed how colour could be used as a unifying element to bring a building together and make it one with its furniture.

Similarly, nothing Dykes Bower designed, decorated or restored in the abbey was approached as an independent feature. All were subservient to a greater whole in which the relationship of diverse elements would be brought into unity. Dykes Bower was not solely attracted to colour; he also delighted in pattern, exemplified in the pavements of the presbytery and the shrine of St Edward the Confessor. This work dated from 1268, when Italian Cosmati workers from Rome laid the pavements of porphyry slabs within red, green and glass mosaic in the form of circles surrounded by ribbons, intertwined or plaited.

In 1957, work began on repairing the lantern and crossing of the nave and transepts. Dykes Bower decided to replace Wyatt's shattered plaster vault with a flat ceiling of mahogany boards, coloured, like those at Norwich and Ely. He filled in the square by decorating the unbroken surface with a design in the form of a quatrefoil enclosed in a diced frame. A bold use of non-pictorial pattern was applied, which reflected the geometrical configuration of the Cosmati pavement below. Butchart and the abbey's painters executed it to be read from a distance in a full range of Gothic colour.

Dykes Bower delighted in small, puzzling work that demanded a close application to detail, and it was this fascination that gave his designs such intensity. The stall canopies on the north side of the King Henry VII Chapel had been dismantled and the woodwork reduced to a collection of hundreds, if not thousands, of pieces, many of them so minute in size that it might have been thought impossible to reassemble them. In 1952, reconstruction began and the fragments were carefully examined, sorted and repaired before being brought together and reassembled in a way that made the canopies stronger than they had been for a very long time.

above: The organ case (one of a pair by J. L. Pearson 1895–7) with colouring by Dykes Bower, 1956–8

Of equal complexity was the reconstruction of Pearson's organ cases. They had been installed in 1895–7, but had been taken down in 1937 for the Coronation of King George VI and put into the triforium. In 1953, after Queen Elizabeth's Coronation, Dykes Bower proposed their restoration and discussed the rebuilding of the instrument to fit them with Sir William McKie, the organist, and Harrison & Harrison, the organ builders. In 1957, the woodwork that had been scattered along the triforium was collected and carefully sorted, and set on the floors of the north apsidal chapels. Two joiners from Longley's pieced the whole together. Much of the elaborate carving was found to be undamaged, very little was missing, but patience and skill were needed to repair the breakages and, from the boxes of small pieces, to find the right one to go back into its intended position.

above: **The ceiling over the crossing**

The ginger colour of their oak did not match the quire stalls, and Dykes Bower believed they would gain from decoration. Changes had to be made to accommodate the rebuilt organ. New outlets for the sound in the cases fronting the aisles improved the musical quality, but it was the gleaming effect visually of Butchart's blue and gold decoration and the silver pipes that made a powerful impression, set against the whiteness of the newly cleaned arcade and vault.

In 1959, Dean Don was succeeded by Dean Abbott, who had previously been Warden of Keble College, Oxford. A less austere man than Don, he was a theologian, closer to Dykes Bower in churchmanship, and wholly susceptible to the increasing enrichment of the abbey's decoration. One of the consequences of re-erecting the newly painted organ cases was the effect they had on the pulpitum, designed in 1828 by Edward Blore. The stylistic diversity of this remarkable assemblage of contradictory elements was fused into a surprisingly successful whole.

Dykes Bower felt it would be improved by colour and 'might then be perceived to have not inconsiderable merit.' The stonework was washed and missing features were made good but Dykes Bower removed the pinnacles, substituting gabled heads that

above: **The restored feretory on the tomb of St. Edward the Confessor**

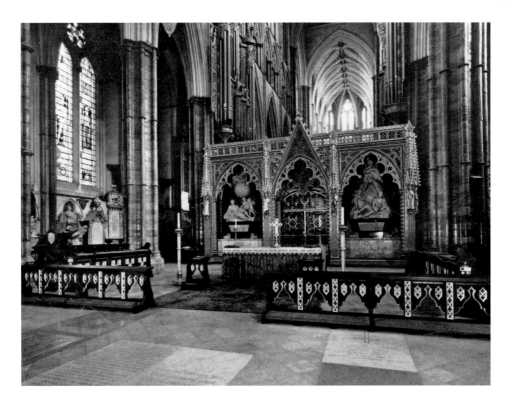

scarcely rose above the level of the parapet; he also reduced the size of the overlarge finial of the central gable, thus enormously improving the scale. The sculptor, Donald Gilbert, modified the six figures.

Many of the patterns were taken from late-medieval precedents in F. C. Eden's sketchbooks, inherited by Dykes Bower in 1944. They were applied to the decoration in gold and colour of the pulpitum. The result is a statement of concentrated richness, in which the architectural members are subtly emphasised by gilding and the delicacy of the carving and sculptural form is, as Dykes Bower predicted, enhanced. Set between piers, the polychromatic colour acted as a foil to the newly polished Purbeck marble. At the same time, the central gable and gates provide a reredos for the altar in the nave. The gilding and colour drew the abbey into unity, emphasising the spatial articulation, the delicacy of proportion and the verticality of the nave and quire, concluding in the octagonal termination of the chancel. The gilded bosses and ribs of the vault were unified with the gilding below. The newly coloured pulpitum magnified the abbey's ceremonial role, and no other work of comparable splendour was executed in a greater English church in the second half of the twentieth century.

above: The new nave altar and furnishings, designed to express the best standards of the Church of England

In 1557, Queen Mary I, during the brief period of Catholic restoration, gave a wooden feretory (a chest for the relics of saints) for the tomb of St Edward the Confessor to replace the one destroyed at the Reformation. It was composed of a blind arcade of Classical arches separated by pilasters, coloured and ornamented with glass. Time had treated it badly, and by 1903 it had become so unsightly that Micklethwaite designed a dramatic pall of red velvet, heavily embroidered in gold, to conceal it; but the feretory had interest as one of the earliest examples, on a miniature scale, of Renaissance design in the country, and that made its restoration desirable. The survival of a measured drawing, made in 1713 by William Talman and annotated with descriptive notes in Latin, proved invaluable in supplementing the indications surviving in the actual structure, which were just enough to show the authentic details of mouldings and carved capitals.

The feretory was taken to Longley's and subjected to scrupulous examination. Few of the glass pieces on the pilasters survived. No matching glass could be found, and their replacements had to be especially made and cut to shape in 10,000 tiny pieces. The pilasters were gilded from behind to give richness to the colour, and were set in especially prepared mastic. A joiner and carver gradually pieced together the innumerable new sections of woodwork, decorated in green and porphyry marbling, both behind glass and directly on the wood, with the mouldings gilded. The feretory had regained the appearance it must once have had, but the colour and glitter threw into stark contrast the defacement of the shrine itself. It was Dykes Bower's ultimate intention to being back to it something of the beauty it had lost, but that plan was never realised.

In 1965, work was resumed on Blore's quire stalls, broadly following the Surveyor Sir Walter Tapper's scheme of gilding with a few minor changes and major additions. Where appropriate, the gold was burnished, the stall backs were painted with a blue diaper pattern, fulfilling Tapper's wishes, and powderings were added to the panels of the organ balustrade above the returned stalls.

At the same time, the reredos, designed by Scott and erected in 1867, was repaired and solidly regilded by Campbell, Smith & Co., with the astonishing number of broken or lost features repaired and reinstated. Much of the detail, as in the tabernacle work above the mosaic panel, is of extraordinary delicacy, a *tour de force* of workmanship. 'To compare this west side of the reredos (with the exception of Salviati's mosaic of the Last Supper) with the east is to be reminded of the value of careful restoration,' Dykes Bower wrote in recognition of Scott's similar approach to his own, 'The new work, clearly derived from evidence on the east side, had created anew the beauty that the old had conspicuously lost. It preserved as a reality what decay and mutilation would otherwise have caused to perish.'

Dykes Bower intensely disliked the incongruity of the Salviati mosaic, and hoped to replace it with a substitute modelled upon the exquisite thirteenth-century retable (the finest piece of panel painting of its date in Northern Europe) now in the abbey museum. He commented: 'The reredos will never look right until this change is accomplished.'

The decoration was coordinated to reach completion in the nonocentenary year

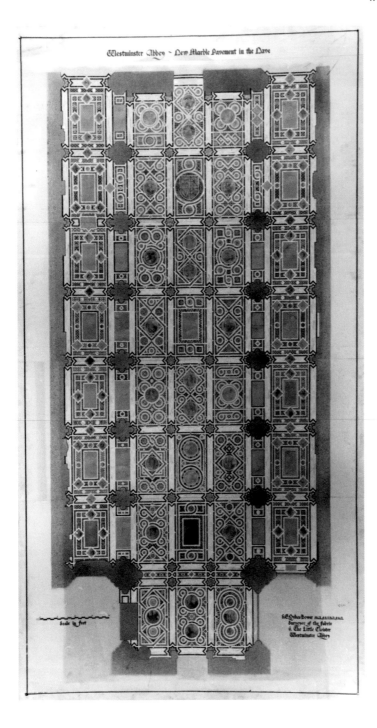

Westminster Abbey ~ New Marble Pavement in the Nave

above: The proposed Cosmati pavement

in 1969. The sanctuary of the nave altar had long been one of Dykes Bower's concerns because it was the first thing to be seen by visitors when they entered. Here, he maintained, the standards of the Church of England should be seen at their best. In 1963 a staircase of wrought iron, made to a previously unexecuted design by W. Bainbridge Reynolds, was added to the sixteenth-century pulpit, and replaced the wooden stairs 'of the meanest kind' designed by Lethaby. A legacy from Dean Don and an anonymous Australian donor enabled the sanctuary to be furnished with stalls, desks, altar rails, fald stools and a credence table, using silky oak and maple presented by the State Government of Queensland.

top: **The Dean's cope made for the 900th anniversary of the foundation of Westminster Abbey**

Dykes Bower once more followed Comper's and Eden's lead and appealed to European precedent:

> Occasions which allow woodwork to be executed in the manner which these gifts made possible for the Abbey are so rare as to be, in present times, almost unprecedented. The combination of fine timber, inlays of maple, ebony and sycamore, and gilding is in the tradition of such magnificent furniture as may be found in the cathedrals of Spain and Italy, but it is hardly to be found in England.

top: The Jerusalem Chamber as restored by Dykes Bower
above: Drawing for proposed textiles for the Dean's cope design

The cleaning, repairing, lighting, restoration, gilding and colouring, and new furniture were a marvel of orchestrated planning. One significant proposal was omitted: the abbey floor.

The floor had been a continual source of worry for a very long time. In 1963 it was estimated that over four million people walked through the abbey yearly, causing damage not only to the paving but, even worse, to the memorial floor slabs, causing a risk of accidents. The hard surface was in many places lost, loosening particles of stone dust as the floor eroded under people's feet and making repair a losing battle. The abbey needed a new floor that would be durable, easy to clean and appropriate to the needs of the building. Compared to normal stone, the black-and-white marble floors in the King Henry VII Chapel and in the quire were almost as good as when they were first laid. Dykes Bower's radical solution was to propose marble for the nave as well.

Westminster Abbey, one of the most outstanding churches of Christendom, is the supreme medieval embodiment of English genius in architecture, yet it is intimately linked with the greatest achievements of France, and the masterpieces of Rome and northern Italy. Following Comper's appeal to European precedent, Dykes Bower believed the abbey should not be seen in narrow, insular terms but acknowledge its debt to the Continent for decoration, furniture and monuments as well as architecture. Scott had emphasised this uniquely important aspect, especially in the floors of the presbytery and feretory.

Dykes Bower argued that the magnificent Cosmati pavings in the Lateran Basilica, S Maria Maggiore and Siena Cathedral had stood the test of time. Despite vast crowds of visitors, the marble floors of St Peter's, Rome, had not deteriorated, nor had those in St Paul's Cathedral. In the Italian examples, the Cosmati pavements extend for the entire floor surface. On a larger scale, Dykes Bower argued, the same principle might once have applied to the abbey. A Cosmati pavement would thus not be an innovation so much as an extension of an existing precedent.

The Dean and Chapter invited him to prepare a design for a new pavement in the nave. It was to be based on the use of marbles selected for their durability and decorative possibilities, which the Cosmati design principles were best suited to developing. All the existing brasses and memorial slabs were worked into the scheme, though their positions had, in most cases, to be changed; ample provision was made for the addition of future memorials; it would cost at least £100,000. The Queen had signified willingness that her gift on the occasion of the nonocentenary year should take the form of that part of the paving which comprised the nave sanctuary. It would be marked by the incorporation of the Royal Arms as the central feature.

On 12 October 1964, a brief notice was published in *The Times* announcing that the plans were in course of preparation and that the Queen had agreed to head the list of contributors. In addition, a grant of £20,000 from the Minister of Public Buildings and Works was approved by the Historic Buildings Council. It was hoped that in 1965 and 1966 further gifts to the abbey would enable the work to be put in hand early in 1967. Then the balloon went up.

Westminster Abbey is a Royal Peculiar, exempt from any jurisdiction other than that of the Sovereign. No advice, beyond royal assent, need be sought for anything that is done to, or put in, it. The government's offer was made shortly before a general election, and the Historic Buildings Council was by no means unanimous. Three members in particular were exercised about the scheme: Nikolaus Pevsner, John Summerson and the Earl of Euston, the Chairman to the Society for the Protection of Ancient Buildings. Meetings of the Council are confidential. Nevertheless, Euston privately informed the SPAB and asked Judith Scott, the Secretary to the Council for the Care of Churches, to send the cutting from *The Times* announcing the scheme to J. M. Richards, the paper's architectural correspondent. Miss Scott wanted the Council for the Care of Churches to protest, but their hands were tied for the same reason as those of the Historic Buildings Council. Richards had, however, been told independently by Euston and Summerson, both of whom were anxious to preserve their anonymity.[7]

Owing to the abbey's independence, Dykes Bower was not obliged to consult the Ancient Monuments Inspectorate of the Ministry of Works, nor at any time during his surveyorship had the Dean and Chapter considered doing so. The Council for the Care of Churches wrote a letter to the Minister, signed by the chairman, expressing their strong disapproval of what was proposed and recommending that no government money should be spent on it. In December, Richards sent a confidential memorandum, written on behalf of the objectors, to the news editor of *The Times*, setting out the facts, identifying the sources of information, and basing the objections on:

a. The unsuitability of a new modern floor aping a past style.

b. The falsity of Dykes Bower's claim that his plan follows what was the original intention with regard to the Abbey floor – there is no historical evidence that such a floor was ever proposed, although patterned marble does exist elsewhere in the Abbey.

c. His plan would mean doing away with the old stone slabs, many of which are part of the original floor laid down in mediaeval times. This they regard as vandalism.[8]

It was a powerful protest. The first objection was Richards's alone but reflected Pevsner's views. The second pursued the official line of the SPAB. The most emotive was the reference to the loss of the medieval slabs. Their age was uncertain. Some might be part of the original floor, but others dated from the eighteenth century. It had been continuously patched and renewed. Despite the historical objections, the Dean and Chapter remained convinced that ultimately the provision of a completely new floor in the nave would have to be faced.

The subject amounted to an obsession with Lord Euston, later the Duke of Grafton, who referred to it in 1995 in an interview for the *Sunday Telegraph*,

'When the Queen, who had made a donation towards repairing the floor, heard what was proposed she put her foot down,' says the Duke of Grafton, who brought the leading architectural historians of the day, Nikolaus Pevsner

and John Summerson, into the fray against Dykes Bower. ... 'He was a ruthless
improver and in the end he was more or less sacked,' recalls the Duke.[9]

This view, unfortunately believed by a number of people, is not supported by the
documentary evidence. The Queen specifically offered her gift for laying the Royal
Arms in front of the pulpitum. Far from being dismissed from the abbey, Dykes Bower
was appointed Surveyor Emeritus on his retirement in 1973. The combined official
pressure was so strong that eventually the abbey acquiesced, agreeing that the masons
must continue patching as before, while Lady Euston, the Mistress of the Robes, had
the unenviable task of returning the Queen's gift. The Duke of Grafton's opposition to
Dykes Bower was not confined to Westminster, but also had an adverse impact on the
progress of work at St Edmundsbury Cathedral.[10]

The Cosmati pavement meant a great deal to Dykes Bower, possibly too much. It
was a sign of confidence suggestive of J. L. Pearson's controversial rebuilding of the
north transept façade in the 1880s. So far, Dykes Bower had achieved his goals with the
unanimous support of the Dean and Chapter without encountering preservationist
objections. Marble was practical and it was the final binding element that would, he
considered, draw the abbey into unity. The Cosmati pavement would be one with the
original in the presbytery, the decoration of the lantern and what he hoped would one
day be a new reredos designed on the same lines.

Dykes Bower's misjudgement in this instance should not prejudice recognition of
his achievement. He loved the abbey, knew it intimately, respected and understood
the work carried out by his predecessors, above all by Scott. The implacable feud
conducted by the SPAB reflected little credit on the Society, and Dykes Bower's work at
Westminster Abbey and elsewhere remains undervalued owing to blinkered prejudice
stemming from these episodes.

The replacement of old roof timbers added another element to the controversy.
They had been restored by Blore in the nineteenth century. Despite the counter-
force of the buttresses, these were pushing the walls outward; they were infested by
beetle and beyond preservation. Conventional practice was to burn ravaged timber
on removal. The decision to do so was made by McKenna Hughes, the Surveyor to
the Roofs, and archaeologists were not given the opportunity beforehand to examine
them. It was Dykes Bower who took the blame for this failure, and the division of
responsibility was not made public. In the ensuing furore nobody felt it necessary to
mention that one bay of the abbey roofs had, in fact, been repaired on strict conser-
vationist principles, leaving evidence of medieval structure for the examination of
archaeologists and antiquarians.[11]

The Surveyor is responsible not only for the abbey church but the precincts, their
curious and varied buildings and gardens of all periods, from the Middle Ages to the
present century. As such, Dykes Bower's restoration of the Jerusalem Chamber was as
momentous as his work elsewhere. The same extent of disrepair found in the abbey
was generally discovered in the precincts, and had to be addressed. The job was almost
impossible for one man.

The strands and principles of workmanship that Dykes Bower drew together and applied went back to the rediscovery of the traditional crafts by Pugin. The connection threaded back from Dykes Bower to Eden and Comper, from them to G. F. Bodley and Thomas Garner, from both to Scott, from Scott to Pugin, from Pugin to George Myers, his builder, and the residual legacy of the medieval stonemasons. At Westminster, Dykes Bower used the best surviving workmen in the conviction that what could be done once can be done again. He did not believe in lost arts. He sought people who could do work and employed them. The young were sometimes astonished by what they were able to achieve under his tutelage. Today there is a resurgence of good workmanship of the highest standard. When Dykes Bower was following his lonely path, it looked as if workmanship applied within a traditional architectural context was dying.

The reason Westminster Abbey remained for long the most atmospheric and least vulgarised of our greater churches is solely due to Dykes Bower. In a tribute on his eightieth birthday in 1983, Gavin Stamp wrote:

> *He has shown a respect for and an understanding of his predecessors' careful*
> *work at the Abbey, and if I at times regret that he sometimes responded*
> *more to the self-confidence of Gilbert Scott in his restoration rather than to*
> *the 'anti-scrape' of W. R. Lethaby, I am convinced by the appropriateness of*
> *every change he has made.*[12]

The long programme of work Dykes Bower set in motion in 1951 remained unfinished when he retired in 1973. A huge volume had been accomplished and he laid the foundations for work continued by his successors, notably the restoration of the stonework of the King Henry VII Chapel.

Notes

1. Letter from Sir John Summerson to Anthony Symondson, 24 January 1992.

2. The quotations in this chapter on Westminster Abbey are taken from the audit reports presented to the Dean and Chapter, written by Stephen Dykes Bower during the years when he was Surveyor. He lent the author copies at the start of work on researching this book because he wanted the narrative to be correct. All facts on his work for the Abbey are taken from them. Dykes Bower papers.

3. Letter from W. I. Croome to F. C. Eeles, 20 January 1953. Eeles papers, Church of England Record Centre. I am grateful to the late Donald Findlay for sending me copies of the Croome–Eeles correspondence relating to Stephen Dykes Bower.

4. Conversation with Winifrid Peppiatt, c.1970.

5. Conversation with Warwick Pethers, c.1995.

6. Anthony Symondson and Stephen Bucknall, *Sir Ninian Comper: an Introduction and Gazetteer*, Reading, Ecclesiological Society and Spire Books, 2006, pp.159–63.

7. Conversation with Sir James Richards, c.1995.

8. A copy of this memorandum, contained in a file, was lent to me by Sir James Richards. It contains a letter from Judith Scott in which she wrote, 'At the request of Lord Euston, I enclose a cutting from "The Times" of 12th October last, on the subject of repaving the floor of the nave. There is no need to return the cutting as we have taken a copy for our file.'

9. See '2m Legacy Sparks Holy Row', by Kenneth Powell, *Sunday Telegraph*, 17 December 1995; and reply by Anthony Symondson in a letter to the editor, *Sunday Telegraph*, 29 December 1995.

10. *The Times*, 3 May 1965, p.5.

11. Letters by Dean Abbott and Stephen Dykes Bower, defending the work done in the roofs, were published in *The Times*, 11 February 1967, and 18 February 1967 (pp.9 and 13 respectively).

12. Gavin Stamp, *Spectator*, 10 April 1983, p.32; 'The English Tradition', *Spectator*, 12 April 1986, pp.20–2.

4 St Edmundsbury Cathedral

The building I should most wish should benefit from the trust money is St Edmundsbury Cathedral, Bury St Edmunds. It has a special place in my affections because I was able to design and carry out the enlargement which, it may be claimed, has visibly confirmed its status as a Cathedral. This was achieved when scarcely anything comparable was being done and at a time when current professional opinion gave no encouragement to stylistic appropriateness but only what spuriously represented itself as 'modern' or 'contemporary'. My rejection of such thinking was based on a belief that more permanent satisfaction and interest would derive from work demonstrating that new work should look, not different, but natural and harmonious; that gave the opportunity for the exercise of skills and crafts-manship not extinct but only neglected and under-used.[1]

Dykes Bower died on 11 November 1994 and left his estate on trust for the completion of St Edmundsbury Cathedral. These words are taken from the first paragraph of a statement appended to his will, drafted for the guidance of the trustees of his estate. It sets out his objectives, explaining the unique character of the building and its place in English post-war architecture.

The Diocese of St Edmundsbury and Ipswich was formed in 1914 and the parish church of St James, Bury St Edmunds, with its large nave of nine bays with wide aisles built in 1503 by John Wastell and standing within the abbey precincts, was consti-tuted the cathedral church. The nave is almost devoid of carving and ornament, but of cathedral proportion and scale. In 1865–9 Sir George Gilbert Scott replaced the original flat-pitched panelled ceiling with an open hammer-beam roof and an aisleless chancel, the third to have been built in the history of the church. As a cathedral the building was unsatisfactory, having only one small chapel and inadequate vestries. The First World War prevented plans for enlargement. Walter Tapper prepared two designs, but the 1929 Depression and the Second World War made it impossible to proceed with either.

Dykes Bower was always conscious of Wastell's distinction as an architect. A local man, he designed the fan vault of King's College Chapel, Cambridge, and the Bell Harry Tower at Canterbury Cathedral as well as notable Perpendicular parish churches in Saffron Walden and Lavenham and the east end of Peterborough Cathedral. Dykes Bower was keen to maintain continuity with his predecessor.

opposite: The north side of St Edmundsbury Cathedral, showing the nave by John Wastell (right), the transept, choir, and west cloister range by Stephen Dykes Bower, completed 1970, the Cathedral Centre (left), by Dykes Bower with the Whitworth Co-Partnership, and the north transept extension, tower and east cloister by Warwick Pethers of the Gothic Design Practice

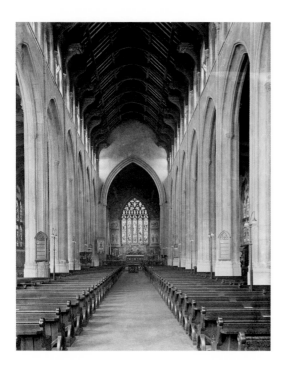

In 1943 he was invited to make a report, and in 1945 was appointed as architect for the extension. He aimed to enlarge and beautify the existing building in such a way that it would be more worthy of its status as the cathedral of the diocese and county. From the beginning, he prepared a coordinated plan, foreseeing the practical needs of a modern cathedral and providing accommodation for them in the right position in an orderly manner.

Dykes Bower thought the nave and aisles were spacious, dignified and finely proportioned. He also thought that the church had been fortunate in being decorated by stained glass of exceptional quality. The nave was glazed by Clayton and Bell; the east window was a good work by John Hardman & Co.; and the chancel had four side windows by C. E. Kempe, three of them early work from 1874 of exquisite beauty, comparable with medieval glass.

He recommended washing the stonework to bring out its natural colour, and limewashing the plaster of the walls. He proposed replacing the nineteenth-century floor of red and blue tiles with a chequer-work pattern of large unglazed floor tiles called pamments in low tones of buff and pink. This would give the opportunity of reviving their production; they were peculiar to Suffolk and were to be found in many churches in the county, although they had not been made for a long time.

The mural tablets would be cleaned and, where necessary, repainted; their heraldic

above: **The cathedral as St James's Church, with the nave roof and chancel**

colours, if missing, would be restored. The font and its late-Gothic cover, designed by F. E. Howard, would be enriched by colour and gilding as the designer intended. The hammer beams and the main structural members of the roof, along with their coats of arms and angels, would be coloured. Scott's chancel was not big enough for cathedral use and it was decided to demolish it, but the principal elements would be preserved for future use. These plans, predating Dykes Bower's activities at Westminster Abbey, were the first of their kind to be comprehensively applied by him to a major English church, demonstrating how mature and accretive at this time was his approach to the treatment of churches and how consistently he regarded St Edmundsbury (as the new diocese was named) as a building to be brought into unity.

When completed in 1949, *The Times* illustrated it and published a glowing reaction by F. C. Eeles:

> *The Cathedral Church of St James has one of the finest fifteenth-century naves in East Anglia ... some excellent work has been done on the nave under the direction of the eminent architect Mr Dykes Bower. He has followed what has been done with such success at King's College, Cambridge, and reverted to medieval precedent by whitening the internal walls and hopelessly stained and dirty stonework. The result is as fine as at Cambridge. The church looks nearly twice its size. Every ray of sunlight is picked up, while the late-Victorian glass – a really good series of windows by Clayton & Bell – is now properly displayed and one realizes how good it is.*
> *The fine hammer beam roof, in strict East Anglian style, though modern, is, like the glass, exceedingly good work of its period. Free from the limitation of 'no conjectural restoration,' now so wisely and generally observed, it has been possible to enliven the enormous expanse of timber by the use of colour and gold in a way not allowable in those churches where the woodwork is ancient.*
> *The visitor can now appreciate the architectural value of this fine church and can realize what it will be like when the full Cathedral scheme is carried out.*[2]

In 1953, plans for the first scheme of enlargement were published. The ruins of the Benedictine abbey and the necessity of preserving a right of way to the abbey gardens precluded any great extension to the east. The existing length of 61 metres (200 feet) could only be increased to 76 metres (248 feet). 'By comparison ... with Ely and Norwich, Bury St Edmunds can never be a big cathedral; but it is neither necessary nor, in view of the cost, expedient that it should be.'

The new quire would therefore be of five bays, with a south aisle of four and a longer north aisle. The main additions would lie to the north, providing, on the ground floor, a sacristy; vestries for the bishop, provost and clergy; room for the wardens, vergers and cleaners; a cathedral office and a chair store. At first-floor level there would be a new chapel – commemorating the meeting of barons at Bury prior to the signature of the Magna Carta in 1215 – over the sacristy and store, chapter house and choir vestries.

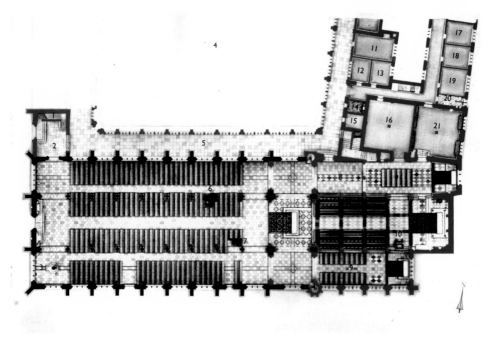

PLAN AT FLOOR LEVEL (*New work shown in red*)

1 Stairs to Library	4 Cloister Garth	7 Lectern	10 Bishop's Throne	13 Vergers	16 Chair Store	19 Clergy Vestry
2 West Porch	5 Cloister	8 Organ Over	11 Cathedral Office	14 Cleaners	17 Bishop's Vestry	20 Lavatory
3 Font	6 Pulpit	9 Chapels	12 Wardens	15 Organ Blower	18 Provost's Vestry	21 Sacristy

The boys' vestry would be large enough for a song school. The Magna Carta Chapel, to be constructed mainly of materials from Scott's chancel, was to be separate from the main part of the cathedral so that services could be held quietly, without restriction to the movement of visitors, on the model of the Lady Chapel at Ely. A cloister would give access to these buildings and to others planned to be built on land not yet owned by the cathedral. A northwest porch would become the chief entrance and would have a parvis for the cathedral library.[3]

Wastell was an architect with a recognisable style of his own, to which Dykes Bower thought it appropriate to pay respect, while giving the new work a character that would align it with the style of the churches of the diocese. 'In such a beautiful town', he wrote, 'and particularly in the setting of this cathedral, with the ruins of the Abbey close by and the great perpendicular church of St Mary alongside, there would be no justification for disregarding the architectural *genius loci*.'

Local character was expressed in building materials, such as knapped flint, already used on the south side of the nave clerestory and applied to the new transepts and

above: The plan as proposed in 1953, with new work in red, including the site of the Magna Carta chapel over nos. 16 and 21

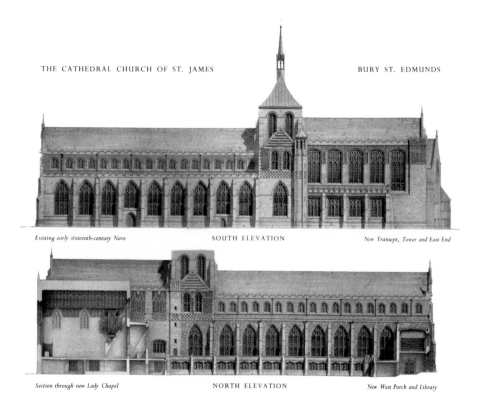

THE CATHEDRAL CHURCH OF ST. JAMES   BURY ST. EDMUNDS

Existing early sixteenth-century Nave   SOUTH ELEVATION   *New Transept, Tower and East End*

Section through new Lady Chapel   NORTH ELEVATION   *New West Porch and Library*

quire. 'The craft of flint-knapping, that so beautified the churches of East Anglia,' wrote
Dykes Bower, 'should not be allowed to perish for lack of the encouragement that such a
project as this may rightly give, and it would be fitting that the building of the cathedral
should be a means of stimulating a local industry.'[4]

Another existing feature that had a formative bearing on the design was the stained
glass. The subjects of the three early windows by Kempe – the Nativity, the Crucifixion
and the Ascension – made them suitable for incorporation in the east window of the
quire. The small amount of glass that would have to be added could without difficulty
be matched to Kempe's work.

The Hardman glass was set in Decorated tracery, and Dykes Bower planned to adopt
it as the east window of the new Magna Carta Chapel and modulate the architectural
expression of the chapel and its vestibule to provide a harmonious setting. In making
the chapel the same size as Scott's chancel, it would be possible to reuse the oak roof.

He wanted to give the low-lying cathedral greater prominence without
overwhelming the Norman tower – one of the former gateways to the monastery –
that, though detached, was part of the cathedral and contained its bells. Its

above: Elevations for the 1953 proposals, with the short tower originally proposed

top: The north side as proposed in 1953, perspective by J D M Harvey
above: The south side of the cathedral, with the Norman bell tower, perspective by J D M Harvey

massiveness made it a dominant adjunct, and only later did Dykes Bower decide to challenge its primacy.

The proposed new tower would rise, not from the ground, but from the intersection of the nave, transept, quire and roofs. Dykes Bower deliberately aimed at the kind of effective contrast, in shape and form, with the bell tower as exemplified by many French cathedrals. The new tower was designed as a lantern with walls little higher than the Norman tower, but the pyramidal roof and flèche of copper would bring the cathedral into view from Angel Hill and other parts of the town.

The demolition of Scott's chancel meant the formation of a new opening to the crossing, disclosing the view of the lantern and the gilded and coloured quire ceiling from the nave. The shape of Scott's hammer-beam roof limited the height to which an arch of the full width of the nave could be carried. Taking his answer from Wastell's work at the east end of the nave of Canterbury Cathedral, Dykes Bower adopted the solution of a strainer arch, supporting a smaller arch above. This smaller arch was broken by tracery, designed to be seen framed within the curve of the hammer beam. The strainer arches acted as a tie, bracing the tower piers and buttressed by new walls between the ends of the aisles and transepts.

above: **The south side before 1939**

In replanning the cathedral precincts, Dykes Bower aimed to create 'not just the ideal surroundings for a cathedral, but a civic improvement that would add notably to the attractions of the town.' He urged a simplified plan for the space between St Mary's and the cathedral. The churchyard, when cleared of 'the confused medley of graves, trees and paths' and replaced by a lawn, would give prominence to the bell tower. 'Nothing indeed could be worse than its present aspect – shapeless, chaotic and overgrown.' A small paved square was planned at the west end to reveal the Norman tower as axial on Churchgate Street, while the early nineteenth-century Athenaeum would become an island. It was an imaginative proposal; as Dykes Bower explained:

> The sequence of Angel Hill and the enlarged Chequer Square, with the
> Athenaeum in between, the cathedral opposite and the cathedral close
> extending down one side of Crown Street as far as St Mary's, would give Bury
> St Edmunds a centre that, scenically and architecturally, would compare with
> the best that other towns can show. Rarely is so great a civic improvement
> capable of achievement with, comparatively, so little alteration.[5]

In 1956, the scheme was launched with an appeal. The total cost was estimated to be £275,000 and that of the first stage £75,000; the main part of the development

above: **Model with amended tower design, 1962**

was planned to be achieved before 1964, the jubilee of the founding of the diocese, a long programme to be achieved stage by stage when funds were available. F. C. Eeles regarded it as a model of what a new cathedral of the Church of England should be, and it was enthusiastically approved and supported by the Cathedral Chapter and Council and the Central Council for the Care of Churches. The bishop and provost thought the enlargement should be of national, if not of international, interest. Few buildings of the time got off to a better start.[6]

If the work had been carried out as Dykes Bower proposed St Edmundsbury would be one of the most complete modern English cathedrals of the second half of the twentieth century, in which provision was made for every contingency of diocesan life. While the Church authorities and the national press welcomed the scheme, it was badly received by influential powers in the architectural press. Foremost in antagonism was the anonymous Astragal column in the *Architects' Journal*, which spoke for the rising Modernist influence in the profession.[7] No detail of Dykes Bower's proposals was spared, for the anonymous writer presumed that either everything should be kept or that much more radical change was appropriate, invoking the recent 'Outrage' special issue of the *Architectural Review* written by Ian Nairn.

above: **Model with amended tower design, 1962**

The fundamental premise behind this attack, the first that Dykes Bower was to suffer, was that work in the Gothic style was, in 1956, indefensible. The design was not only dismissed as an anachronism, but no attempt was made to explain Dykes Bower's clearly set out reasons; they were deliberately obfuscated, and considered dismissible.

Dykes Bower had not only offended against Modernism, but also against the taste for 'pleasing decay', the elegant melancholia of the neglected churchyard, sculpture shaped by the elements, the texture given by time, the English sense of place that contradicted Dykes Bower's liking for order and neatness. Some older traditionalist architects were treated more respectfully, but Dykes Bower was too young for his views to be allowed to pass unopposed.

The response from the county was sluggish. Edmund Vestey, whose family, owners of the Dewhurst and Fray Bentos meat wholesale brands, also funded the central tower of Liverpool Cathedral, enabled the crossing and the base of the tower to be built. Work started in 1960 and was sufficiently advanced for the crossing and quire to be consecrated in 1970 but, once these were done, the bishop – claiming the greater need of foreign missions allied with local opposition – declared the appeal closed and building at an end. The opposition was led by the Duke of Grafton, Dykes Bower's adversary in

above: **The Lady Chapel with iron screen by Norman Furneaux**

the 1960s at Westminster Abbey, whose seat, Euston Hall, is close to Bury St Edmunds. When the completion of the tower seemed possible in the 1990s, he told Kenneth Powell: 'It is very bad news indeed ... I never approved of Dykes Bower. What he did at Bury is rather un-English.'[8]

Despite these biased and widely disseminated views, furnishing and decoration continued when possible, but certain decisions made by the provost and Cathedral Council ensured that some of the finest parts of the design could never be carried out.

The principal casualty was the abandonment of the Magna Carta Chapel. It was broken from the model by the Very Revd Raymond Furnell, the provost, and the carefully stored roof and mullions from Scott's chancel were sold, making execution of the plans impossible. In 1990 a greatly modified design for a cathedral treasury, incorporating a song school, new vestries, a refectory and meeting rooms, was built to the north in a way that effectively prevented any opportunity of carrying out Dykes Bower's original proposals. While he was responsible for the exterior design and elevations, he was allowed no control over the interior; executive architects, the Whitworth Co-Partnership, carried this out.

above: The north chapel screen, incorporating salvaged Victorian ventilation grilles, and decorated ceiling

At St Edmundsbury the design was evolutionary, not static or imitative. The perspectives illustrating the appeal were not final; modifications and expansion continued from the start of work in 1960. This is seen most noticeably in the evolution of the crossing and tower, both of which were changed from the original scheme of 1956.

Reginald Kirby worked closely with Dykes Bower on the complex design of the two western piers for the tower and the completion of the eastern pair; the north and south tower arches; the western arch, with its gallery in the thickness of the wall above for access to the remaining parapets; and the preparation of the north transept gallery over the cloister roof. As work progressed after Kirby's death the design evolved, and Hugh Mathew, whose role in the practice is described in chapter 7, recommended a considerable increase in the girth and scale of the tower piers. One of the main problems to emerge was the unification of Wastell's Perpendicular window tracery in the nave with Scott's curvilinear tracery that Dykes Bower was using for the east windows.

The extension had to be considered in its local context, which dictated the choice of Romanesque detail in the upper levels of the transept for its reference to the Norman bell tower. However, by heightening the crossing tower and making it the principal unifying feature these disparate elements could fuse together, emphasising the place of the cathedral in Bury by making its presence visible.

above left: The crossing from south to north, showing the north transept gallery completed in 2005
above right: Steps from the cloister to the north porch

The first modification to provide for a tall tower was made in 1962. The termination of the flèche was unchanged, rising from a pyramidal roof of lead and continuing the contrast in scale and form with the bell tower. The elevation needed to bind the increased height with the pyramid and clock faces positioned immediately below the parapets.

These proposals were expensive, and for the time being the crossing was capped by a flat roof. At a later period, Dykes Bower was asked to submit designs for a cheaper alternative. This had to be lower but it retained the flèche. When the design was submitted to the Cathedrals Advisory Committee and the Royal Fine Art Commission, Dykes Bower was told to omit the flèche but privately he declined to do so. The design was elaborated until it reached a final form. Some have supposed that the tower was the folly of overambition committed by Dykes Bower in old age. This was not so: he came to see the inadequacy of the first proposals and attempted to disentangle their disparities.

When the crossing and quire were consecrated in 1970, much in the interior remained unfinished. From the start, decorative ironwork was included in the drawings as an enrichment that would 'impart to the whole internal aspect of the building an increased feeling of size and distance.'[9] Screens made by Norman Furneaux, painted red and gold, were added to the chapels, and the altars were furnished with silk frontals and hangings. One screen in particular was remarkable and surprisingly effective for being made of metal grilles from a heating system in a Manchester church, placed diagonally within a wrought-iron setting. In 1984, a sunburst of wrought iron and semi-precious stones made by Furneaux to Dykes Bower's design was placed in the apex of the arch behind the high altar to commemorate the cathedral's seventieth anniversary. But it was a slow and laborious process in which only fragmentary parts of Dykes Bower's overall scheme were carried out, although enough was finished to show the richness of effect of the whole.

The future of St Edmundsbury had preoccupied Dykes Bower ever since the appeal was closed in 1970, causing him to bequeath the greater part of his estate to enable work to continue. Knowing that the extent of the estate would be little more than £2 million, he directed that the completion of the north transept should have first call on the funds that his bequest might make possible, because it would easily be overlooked and also because the bequest would adequately pay for it.

Dykes Bower did not specify that the bequest was to be used for the tower, but he stated that he regarded it as an essential architectural feature: 'The utmost height is, however, desirable. The cathedral is situated in the lowest part of the town and neither from the surrounding country nor among the streets is its presence noticeable. Bury St Edmunds, though now a cathedral town, offers little sign of it.'[10]

Dykes Bower's death in 1994 coincided with the appointment of a new provost, later the first dean, the Very Revd James Atwell. Public money was more freely available than in 1970, and the bequest provided a practical possibility that the tower might be completed from independent sources at the same time as the north transept. A successful bid to the Millennium Commission, combined with the legacy,

enabled both to be completed at the same time, a remarkable achievement in view of the lingering hostility to the integrity of design and constructional standards that it represented.

Many considered Dykes Bower's final tower design a foreign element in an East Anglian town, and few were keen to see it executed. The first application to the Millennium Commission was refused and a second submission – a short, stunted tower with crenellations in the manner of Dykes Bower's compromise design – was then submitted, despite having been created to show what should not be done. This too was in process of rejection when the impasse was resolved in a surprising way.

The obvious alternative to the spire was to use the more conventional termination of corner pinnacles. Warwick Pethers, who had been appointed by the Dykes Bower Will Trust to work initially on the north transept, prepared a design in which the upper levels of the tower were influenced by three precedents: G. F. Bodley's tower at Long Melford (1903), George Gilbert Scott Junior's grand and elegant tower at Cattistock, in Dorset (1876), combined with elements taken from Wastell's Bell Harry Tower at Canterbury, (1490–1515). This was a creative use of precedent within the Dykes Bower tradition, and sprang from the design of the stem of the tower. Having been shown to a small circle of

above: **The north transept gallery amd new cloister bays by Warwick Pethers**

sympathisers, the new design was published, linking it with Hugh Mathew's name, in an article by Marcus Binney in *The Times*.[11] Mathew himself designed an alternative crowned by an octagon. The published proposal looked so obviously right that it was well received by the provost, and this time the Millennium Lottery bid was successful. Prince Charles agreed to become patron of the appeal and described the project as a 'spiritual beacon for the new millennium'; it was the only specifically Christian project supported by the commission, consisting not only of the tower but a package of work that was intended to further the completion of the cathedral.

Pethers had started with two assistants, Eric Cartwright and Robin Gladden, working in a cottage within sight of the great but unfinished tower of Lavenham church. With Mathew he then established the Gothic Design Practice, and it was moved to the upper floor of the old Gibson's Bank in the market place at Saffron Walden, a building by W. E. Nesfield much admired by Dykes Bower for its enormous lead gutters, second only, he considered, to those at Canterbury Cathedral. From here, Pethers administered the £10 million building contract. Pethers and Mathew were joined by Abd al Halim Orr, a recent graduate of the Prince of Wales's Institute for Architecture where an exhibition of Dykes Bower's drawings was held in 1996. Help with presentation drawings was provided by Chris Draper, Pamela Hutchin, Andrey Serov and Edwin Venn.

In all, more than 3,000 drawings were produced – considerably more than would have been required in Victorian or even in Dykes Bower's times. There were several reasons for this. The specific circumstances of the project – notably the fact that Dykes Bower had chosen to leave his money in trust rather than to the cathedral, and the cathedral's ambivalent response to the tower design which had by then elicited a £5 million grant from the Millennium Commission – meant that the scheme design drawings had to have the precision of legal documents. Secondly, there had been an enormous proliferation in the number of committees whose approval was required. Thirdly, there were the cathedral's requirements for competitive tendering and absolute cost certainty. Finally, to give everyone on site the best possible chance of getting their work right first time – whether or not they had ever done anything similar before – every 't' was crossed and every 'i' dotted. As a result, it became possible to add work not originally part of the project, including a stone interior for the tower and most of the east walk of the cloisters.

The second way in which this campaign of building differed from that of the 1960s was in its use of more conservative building techniques. Dykes Bower had never been hidebound in his use of structural skills, and Kirby had seen that reinforced concrete could be used to make Gothic slenderer even than Perpendicular. However, well within Dykes Bower's lifetime the shortcomings of some modern materials and their execution were becoming apparent. Luckily, the conservation movement had by then done much to rediscover traditional materials and means to achieving one's purpose, to the point that it was possible to build the tower in loadbearing mass masonry set in lime mortar as Wastell would have done in the fifteenth century.

A triumph of the tower project is the Barnack stone of which it is built: warm and variegated in colour, shelly in texture, and more durable than any other limestone. To Dykes Bower this had always been the Holy Grail of building stones, but no new supplies had been available since the Middle Ages, when they had been exhausted in the building of Ely and Peterborough cathedrals and other monastic buildings, including Bury St Edmunds. In the 1960s, Dykes Bower had used Doulting stone to emulate its appearance and Clipsham its durability. When the time came to tender for the stone, Paul Wilkinson, the quantity surveyor of Gleeds, said that to obtain genuinely competitive tenders it was essential not to name the stone. Accordingly, when asked, Pethers named only the desirable but long unobtainable Barnack, to which Dykes Bower had so often referred. To everyone's surprise, the successful tenderer, stonemason, Andre Vrona, telephoned to say that he had discovered an unworked seam of Barnack near Peterborough. He and his colleagues undertook the quarrying, sawing, working and laying of all the stone for the entire project. Carving was done by Peter Kellock and Andy Tanser; the structural engineer was Brian Morton, and the main contractor Bluestone.

Hugh Pearman, the architectural correspondent to *The Sunday Times*, vividly reported the excitement of the project:

> *Carved stone has been laid upon carved stone, to precise tolerances. Flints have been knapped. Men have mixed lime mortar, not cement, to join them. Concrete has been poured – as the Romans did – but not reinforced concrete, and it is no more visible than the bricks that form the cores of the four-feet-thick walls. Carpenters have done solid work in oak. This tower, plus a new transept, extended cloister and two new chapels, are designed to last 1000 years. They have cost £10 million. They just don't do buildings like this anymore.*[12]

On 22 July 2005, the Prince of Wales officially opened the 'Millennium Project', including the tower with its gilded weathervanes and crocketed pinnacles, flint flushwork battlements and stepped buttresses. In 2007, with the project on budget with 97 per cent of the work complete, the result was seen as a triumph of design and structure that immediately became the emblem of the town. Only the eastern range of the cloister needed completion, the fan vault in the tower designed by Hugh Mathew waited to be installed, and the Chapel of the Apostles looked forward to its altar, reredos, hanging pyx and screens, all of which had been designed by Pethers. This remaining endeavour could have been successfully completed and a final programme had been agreed, but bad relations, inherited from Dykes Bower's lifetime, had developed during the course of building. The Fabric Advisory Committee contained few who were sympathetic to Dykes Bower's work, and some members of the Chapter disliked it. In addition, Pethers had inherited Dykes Bower's

opposite: **The north transept and stair, St. Edmundsbury Cathedral, by Dykes Bower and Warwick Pethers**

perfectionism and strength of will. The work had to be right or it was not worth doing at all.

In 2006, Dean Atwell was translated to the Deanery of Winchester and succeeded by the Very Revd Neil Collings, Acting Dean of Exeter, described in his obituaries as one who was able to make 'hard decisions and grasp nettles'.[13] Despite the little work that remained to be done, Collings was determined to dismiss Pethers and one of his first acts was to convene a meeting at which this object was the first item on the agenda. The motion was carried and Pethers was discharged, amid contradictory press reports.

The Cambridge architect, Henry Freeland, was appointed his successor, and during the three years of Dean Collings's time modified versions of the original designs were executed. Hugh Mathew's fan vault was carved by computer rather than by eye, looking mass-produced with incorrect colouring, oil gilding and lacking the sparkle of powderings. Alan Rome, who was earlier in Dykes Bower's Westminster Abbey office, designed two organ cases with pedestrian pipe shades and weak brattishing, and when installed in 2010 these were decorated by John Bucknall in a palette of colour and *trompe-l'oeil* inimical to Dykes Bower's own colouring in the cathedral. Dykes Bower had in fact wanted the quire stalls, organ tribune and cases to be executed in limed oak that would have turned the quire and sanctuary into a visual unity. In contradiction to Dykes Bower's instructions to the trust, the Chapel of the Apostles was meanly furnished with no thought of screens. None of these modifications was necessary, Dykes Bower would not have approved of them, and they diminish the cathedral's interior as a unified whole. Yet the tower achieves all that it set out to do and not only gives Bury St Edmunds a magnificent skyline seen from Angel Hill but also turns it into a recognisable cathedral town with the Anglican cathedral – surely the last of such structures to be built – at its centre. Few could now imagine it not being there. From whatever vantage point, it vindicates the use of the Gothic style and adds monumental beauty to one of the loveliest towns in East Anglia.

As a work of architecture, St Edmundsbury stands alone among its contemporaries as a living statement of the Gothic style and is, with the exception of Sir Giles Gilbert Scott's Liverpool, the best of the twentieth-century English cathedrals. It is a coda at the end of the century to the magnificent optimism of Liverpool, designed on a different scale and with magnified objectives at the start. Both buildings demonstrate the validity of designing in the Gothic style by demonstrating its infinite, elastic capabilities. Gothic is the architecture of common sense. Scott and Dykes Bower demonstrated that Gothic is distinct from medievalism and has perennial application. St Edmundsbury is not merely a monument to a superseded era; it is a practical model of what can be accomplished as an alternative to transient expedients that fail to satisfy subconscious and aesthetic expectations. The cathedral is an essential link in the chain of architectural continuity.

Notes

1   Stephen Dykes Bower's instructions for his trustees, 8 July 1988.

2   *The Times,* 23 August 1949, p.7; Stephen Dykes Bower, 'The Scheme of Development', appeal brochure, Bury St Edmunds, 1945.

3   *The Times*, 17 October 1956, p.12.

4   Stephen Dykes Bower, 'The Scheme of Enlargement', Bury St Edmunds, 1956.

5   ibid.

6   *The Times*, 22 July 1957, p.5; *Builder*, 14 June 1957, p.722.

7   *Architects' Journal*, 19 April 1956, p.369.

8   See '£2m Legacy Sparks Holy Row', by Kenneth Powell, *The Sunday Telegraph,* 17 December 1995, and reply by Anthony Symondson in a letter to the editor, *The Sunday Telegraph*, 24 December 1995.

9   *The Times*, 24 September 1970, p.12; Stephen Dykes Bower's instructions for his trustees, 8 July 1988.

10   Instructions for trustees, *op. cit.*

11   *The Times*, 26 July 1997, p.11.

12   *The Sunday Times*, 13 March 2005.

13   Obituary by Peter Townley, *Independent*, 21 July, 2010.

5 New Buildings and Major Alterations

St John's, Newbury

In 1955, Dykes Bower was given St John's, Newbury, to rebuild after the destruction during the war of the original church by William Butterfield. War-damage compensation limited the design and was partly responsible for the choice of the Romanesque style, executed in brick. It was built by Musselwhite & Son of Basingstoke and consecrated in 1957. 'I felt justified in using coloured bricks, as Butterfield would have done, while trying to achieve the greatest effect with space, proportion and design', Dykes Bower wrote to James Bentley, adding: 'In the quality of the brickwork, its pointing and so on, I was obviously inspired by Lutyens.'[1]

St John's distantly echoes the plan of G. F. Bodley's St Augustine's, Pendlebury, Manchester, but with noticeable amendments. The wide nave and narrow passage aisles lead to a broad sanctuary. There are structural divisions in the form of arches, which lead at the west from a gabled narthex, containing the baptistery and choir stalls, into the nave; and at the east into a lateral sanctuary. The roofs of the narthex and sanctuary are higher than that of the nave, and define their own spatial compartments. Externally the east end balances the west, and from it on the north and south sides project a chapel and vestries. The aisles run beneath a double clerestory into the sanctuary and continue as a low processional path behind the high altar. They are compressed within a triple eastern arcade and walls, from which rise external buttresses to support the massive eastern bulwark. St John's was built as a church of eucharistic worship where the congregation is brought into visual relationship with the altar by the elimination of choir stalls at the east end.

The stark monumentality of the interior is alleviated by colour and geometrical pattern. The nave ceiling is decorated in heraldic colours with lozenges, and these patterns continue on the sanctuary ceiling and onto the decoration of the tester suspended above the high altar. This is painted with a dove, symbolising the Holy Ghost, contained in an overall geometrical pattern executed in blue, red and gold. Painted brackets with Baroque profiles define the bays. Geometrical patterning is continued in the grisaille glass, and the same motifs are applied in the light screens of wrought iron in which lozenges are incorporated within the volutes. The richest patterns are to be found in the bonded brick, notably in the recessed panels of the sanctuary that repeat the rhythm of the fenestration. The altar – long, low and solidly built of brick – is raised to eye level and is dignified by silver ornaments made by Frank Knight to Dykes Bower's design, and panelled frontals of silk made by Watts & Co.

opposite: St John's, Newbury, Berkshire, 1954–7, south side

It is in the exterior massing that the monumental qualities of St John's are seen to full advantage. The gabled west end has batterings reminiscent of the west end at All Saints, Hockerill (see chapter 1), with the same function of providing a massive prelude to the nave. It combines classical abstraction with Gothic construction. The ground-level storey is pierced with oeil-de-boeuf windows, and these run round the lower walls of the entire church; three vertical panels are built of diapered brick and rise to the level of the parapet. The gable is pierced by a bell opening, and porches are contained within the north and south buttresses.

The east end is equally powerful. The roof and upper walls of the sanctuary are placed, like a box of light perforated by double lancets in round-headed arches, upon the lower levels of chapel, vestries and lateral buttresses rising from the walls of the processional path. It is as satisfying in elevation as the west end. Both extremities flank the bulk of the nave and aisles. Pantiles on the roofs unify these elements, and these add to the rich texture of the patterned bricks.

top: St John's, Newbury, Berkshire, west front

top: St John's, Newbury, interior, looking east

top: St John's, Newbury, shortly after completion
above left: St John's, Newbury, sanctuary shortly after completion
above right: St John's, Newbury, glass in triforium of choir, partly composed of fragments from the bombed church on the site

Dykes Bower saw St John's as a compromise brought about by adverse circumstances, but it remains a major achievement. As well as giving it a colour plate, the revised Berkshire *Buildings of England* is more understanding than its predecessor, calling it 'a learned and poetic design, with more originality and power than most "progressive" churches.'[2] His literate response to a style dictated by the choice of materials testifies to the richness of Dykes Bower's architectural language. St John's, which was among the first post-war buildings in England to be listed, is not a reactionary building but continues an existing architectural tradition and is a serious work of architecture.

Church and College Designs

St Chad's, Middlesbrough, preceded St John's in 1953–7 and the Good Shepherd, Cambridge, followed in 1957–64. Both are modest works, built against economic odds, illustrating the possibilities of brick. St Chad's is small and compact, composed of a nave with aisles and a well-massed exterior but without a chancel. Stylistically it is more dependent on G. E. Street than Bodley, with unmoulded arcades rising from square piers. Against the east wall originally rose a dorsal of red silk, hanging beneath a late-Gothic canopy suspended above a long, dignified altar furnished with a tall crucifix and six candlesticks made by Frank Knight; the roof of the sanctuary is decorated in colour.

The Good Shepherd awaits the completion of a tower and spire. It was summarily dismissed by Pevsner as 'reactionary to a degree almost unbelievable in 1957–8' and harshly condemned in 1964 by one of his pupils in *Cambridge New Architecture*. 'Admittedly the church … is an embarrassment,' wrote Nicholas Taylor, 'in the sort of gimcrack which compromised the Church of England after the great Victorians last designed in Gothic with passion and sincerity. The gloomy, dark brick building … seems weird compared with other new churches in Cambridge, let alone those on the Continent. It displays Romanesque in the nave arcade, seventeenth-century Gothic in the windows, and early twentieth-century Anglican good taste in the interior décor.' Taylor had held reservations about Dyke Bower's work since his schooldays at Lancing, but whatever may be thought of it, it is not gimcrack, being neither cheap or showy, nor is it insincere.

Dykes Bower worked for several Cambridge colleges, restoring Victorian painted decoration at Queens' (see chapter 6) and St John's, and making repairs to older fabric at Magdalene. Following the completion of his repainting scheme at Queens', the Fellows commissioned him in 1955 to design a new range of rooms, the Erasmus Building, for the college, which would have finished Walnut Tree Court, looking directly onto the river. The result was a building of four storeys, for which two different elevational treatments are shown on the drawings. One was in patterned brick, with shallow recessed window bays separated by pilasters with zigzag patterns for capitals; the other was in the Queen Anne style, using a giant order. Both having tall, shafted chimneystacks; a pitched tiled and gabled roof; and mullioned, traceried windows divided by glazing

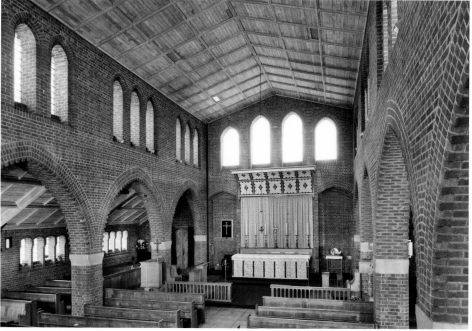

top: St Chad's, Middlesborough, 1953–7
above: St Chad's, Middlesborough, 1953–7

bars. The design was welcomed by the senior Fellows, but was considered dated by their juniors who wanted a Modernist building. Adaptations were made, but were destined for failure.

When the designs were published they excited controversy, and the day before a college meeting, summoned to consider the revised designs, the model was stolen from the college buildings by students from the Cambridge School of Architecture. Dykes Bower resigned and a building on the site was commissioned from Sir Basil Spence. Thus ended his major opportunity to design a new building for a secular use.

Similar problems affected his proposals for adapting the early nineteenth-century Master's Lodge at Magdalene to modern requirements. Younger Fellows were determined on a new, Modernist design, and the commission was later given to one of them, David Roberts, who taught at the School of Architecture. Following the failure of its flat roof, it was given a pitched one at a later date.

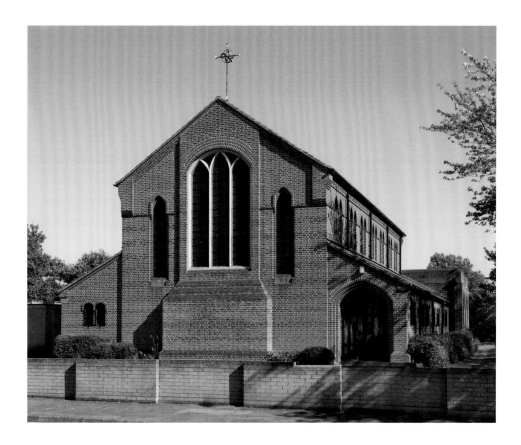

above: **The Good Shepherd, Arbury, Cambridge, west end, 1957–64**

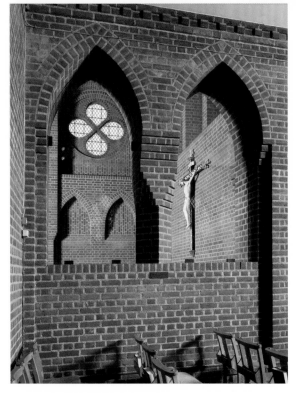

top: The Good Shepherd, Arbury, interior
above: The Good Shepher, Arbury, view into Sanctuary from Lady Chapel

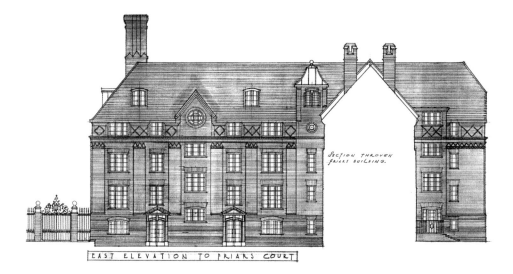

St Nicholas, Great Yarmouth

St Nicholas, Great Yarmouth, Norfolk, is the largest medieval church in England.
During the Commonwealth it had been divided into three churches, one for each sect of
worshippers then using it, and this arrangement survived until the nineteenth century
when the church became undivided for the first time in 200 years. It was reduced to a
shell during the war in a fire raid on 14 June 1942, which destroyed everything except

top: Queens' College, Cambridge, design for new rooms in Walnut Tree Court, 1950
above: Queens' College, Cambridge, perspective of new bulding drawn by Alan Rome

top: St Nicholas's, Great Yarmouth, Norfolk, before bomb damage, restored by J.P. Seddon, 1859–64
above   St Nicholas's, Great Yarmouth, 1953–69, looking west, showing modified arcades

the walls, arcades and tower; the church stood an unkempt ruin for 15 years, and very little of the interior survived. Dykes Bower wanted to make a fresh start and applied a radical approach, structurally and in planning.

He divided the church into two parts by making a new sanctuary in the crossing. In summer the nave, aisles and chapels could be used as a single space. In winter the small, regular congregation was moved into the chancel, which became a church within a church. A collegiate seating plan was made with the altar at the east end.

Using the medieval plan, Dykes Bower set up large chapels to the north and south of the chancel, sparsely furnished to emphasise spatial clarity. Rattee & Kett, the contractors, presented a carved triptych of the Nativity to the Lady Chapel. They had kept the carving for 50 years, waiting to work on a church large and noble enough in which to install it to the best effect. Late-Gothic was adopted as a style, but the restoration was an exercise in modern Gothic rather than pastiche or a conjectural exercise based on what might originally have been there. The arches under the Norman tower were replaced in order to carry the additional weight of a new peal of 13 bells. Dykes Bower considered that the arcades at St Nicholas had too many arches and merged every two original bays into a new wider one, provoking later criticism. New arcades with fine mouldings were designed for the nave and chancel, which halved the number of bays and doubled their size. Steel tie bars and reinforced concrete enabled this to happen and allowed clear, spatial views across the great width of the church. Extra columns and arches were built in the side chapels to improve the proportions.

What Dykes Bower proposed exemplified the standards (following in the wake of J. N. Comper's early liturgical experiments and aesthetic) that the Central Council for the Care of Churches had tried to apply to all Anglican churches, irrespective of style and date. The wooden ceilings glowed with diapered patterns in scarlet, blue, black and white. Hangings and frontals of figured silk, made by Watts & Co., dignified the altars, and the chapels were divided from the chancel by painted Classical screens of wrought iron. An organ, acquired from St Mary, The Boltons, in Kensington, occupied the north transept with a Gothic case decorated with gilding and polychromatic treatment in the traditional East Anglian style. The limed wood also followed East Anglian precedent and was left light with the intention that it would turn silver with time, like the timber in the Perpendicular wool churches close to the east coast. Brian Thomas designed the east window, but Dykes Bower thought that it showed that his work was unsuitable for Gothic churches. Thomas's window in the south transept showed Galilean scenes juxta-posed with aspects of the Yarmouth herring-fishing industry.[4]

A notable feature of St Nicholas is the set of five colossal iron screens forged by the Norfolk blacksmiths, Eric Stevenson, the best English blacksmith of his time, and Bob Blake, his assistant. Stevenson came from a family of smiths going back 200 years in Wroxham, on the Norfolk Broads, and came to Dykes Bower's attention when he was designing gates and screens for Norwich Cathedral and St Martin-in-the-Fields, Westminster. Fifteen tonnes of iron and £4,000 went into the Great Yarmouth screens.

They took six years to cast and beat out, and three weeks to erect. Furthermore, it took the workmen three days simply to carry the pieces into the church.

The citation for Stevenson's Gold Medal awarded by the Blacksmith's Company for the work at St Nicholas declared that 'The cumulative knowledge of four generations finds expression in superb workmanship, with a motif of acanthus leaves and scroll work forming part of the elegant design.'[5]

The interior is marked by understated excellence and order, displaying beauty, taste, good workmanship, scholarship, delicate colouring and detail. St Nicholas was planned to serve the needs of a modern congregation, demonstrating that a centrally planned altar, following Comper's later liturgical experiments, could be accomplished without doing violence to an existing building. It is a model restoration of a major medieval church, adapted to the needs of a flourishing seaport and holiday resort.

However, the work met with unexpected reactions that did Dykes Bower's reputation lasting damage, including a conference paper by the architect George Pace in 1962 and a particularly hostile entry by Pevsner in *The Buildings of England*.[6] In recent years, divisions and subdivisions for functions new to churches, such as book and coffee shops, have confused the interior, trivialising and destroying the controlled flow of space and unity that originally was one of the best features of the church. In 1995, an over-scaled, incongruous painting of the Last Supper, by John Dashwood, was suspended above the nave altar, which also adds nothing to the unity of the interior.

top: St Nicholas's, Great Yarmouth, detail of organ case, painted by Campbell Smith & Co
opposite: St Nicholas's, Great Yarmouth, Lady Chapel with screens by Eric Stevenson

Lancing College Chapel, Lancing, West Sussex

Lancing College Chapel is one of the greatest architectural achievements of the Gothic Revival. In 1868, 13 years after the death of its designer, R. C. Carpenter, work began under his partner William Slater and was continued by his son. The chapel symbolised the religious aspirations of Canon Nathaniel Woodard, a leading educational reformer, and is the supreme monument to the Oxford Movement, greater perhaps than William Butterfield's Keble College, Oxford. Woodward described it as an 'immemorial creed in stone'.

above: Lancing College, perspective of completed west end and unbuilt antechapel, drawn by Alan Rome

The style is French thirteenth-century Gothic in detail but fifteenth-century in proportion, embodying the phase of early French Gothic that connects Westminster Abbey with the Early English Gothic. Woodard insisted on running up the east end to its full height of 30 metres, or 98 feet (only Westminster, York Minster and Liverpool Cathedral are higher), in order to prevent any mutilation of the finished design. Built of Sussex sandstone and vaulted from end to end, the space was slowly extended for a total of nine bays, measuring 44 metres (145 feet), composed of an arcade of clustered columns supporting a triforium and clerestory. The broad nave made an unbroken vessel of space flanked by narrow aisles.

'The outside is magnificent', wrote Pevsner, 'with the imitative detail carried off by the total romantic effect, a Gothic chapel as Turner might have imagined it in paint or Mendelsohn might have personified it in music.[7] Yet Lancing is not merely histrionic scene painting but a controlled exercise in the structural logic of Gothic. The exterior is flanked by flying buttresses that, with the vault, demonstrate a profound understanding of the highly developed system of Gothic construction. The interior is not dramatic so much as aspiring, quiet, unified and gentle, culminating in the long high altar raised on many steps beneath the chord of the apse, thus attesting to its function as a church of eucharistic worship.

above: Left to right: Mr Sheppard (Longleys, builders), Stephen Dykes Bower, Basil Handford, Ian Beer (Head Master), c. 1976

Lancing Chapel was dedicated in 1911, a bare, austere skeleton, lacking the final bay to the west but enriched over time on a restrained English model, developing into a building of faultless beauty. Comper's proposal for the high altar and a great altar screen of tabernacle work delineated in decorated wood remained unexecuted, but he and other architects contributed harmoniously to the gradual furnishing of the chapel during the first three quarters of the twentieth century.

In 1928, Sir George Oatley made designs for the west end and a south-western transept modelled on Westminster Abbey with a vaulted tripartite porch giving access also to Temple Moore's memorial cloister and the crypt. These proposals would have made a sweeping termination, balanced the apse and linked the chapel with Carpenter's school buildings; but they were overambitious in the changed economic circumstances after the First World War, and it seemed that Lancing Chapel was to remain one of the many unfinished churches truncated by that conflict.

In 1946, Canon Arthur Browne-Wilkinson, the Provost of Lancing College, gathered a small group representing different interests in the Woodard Schools. Urgent repairs were needed, and it was decided to form a body of Friends of Lancing Chapel with the task of finishing, as well as maintaining, the building. In 1947, Dykes Bower was appointed architect and the Friends gave themselves until the centenary year of 1968 to raise £100,000, which was at that time the estimated cost.[8]

above left: Lancing College Chapel, hanging lights
above right: Lancing College Chapel, the interior looking west with the organ case by Alan Rome, pulpitum, west bay and rose window by Dykes Bower

An appeal was enthusiastically launched in 1952. John Summerson, who gloried in Carpenter's 'heresy' of refusing to adapt to any progressive 'spirit of the age', was used as a consultant and approved Dykes Bower's proposals. In 1955, Canon Adam Fox, the Archdeacon of Westminster, described in the *Lancing College Magazine* how the completion would work towards its climax:

> *The West front with its tall gable and great rose window will be seen, and*
> *at last it will emerge. The work of art will be nearing completion. But there*
> *is yet the Western ante-chapel and the arch that leads to the entrance. The*
> *ante-chapel though it seems low compared to the main building will never-*
> *theless be a very spacious and somewhat unusual feature, a worthy prelude*
> *and entry to the great church, and not unfitting as a symbol of the Founder's*
> *will fulfilled. The more so, seeing that he ordered that every boy was to be*
> *taught George Herbert's 'Church Porch'. This ante-chapel or narthex will be*
> *much more striking than the rather conventional South West door seen in*
> *Carpenter's drawings.*[9]

Carpenter's plans had dictated Oatley's proposals; Dykes Bower moved a change although not a radical departure, as he described to Basil Handford, the Head of Classics at the school and his main supporter:

> *One point that I think might be worth making is that all the main elements*
> *in the rose window were already in the clerestorey windows – notably the*
> *rather unusual form of the central roundel containing the Lancing arms.*
> *This and the other roundels are to the same scale as their counterparts in*
> *the clerestorey windows and the remarkable thing was, how, in the geometry*
> *of the rose, they seemed to come together quite inevitably in the rose window;*
> *the result is due to its identifying itself so closely with what existed.*[10]

Dykes Bower's plan provided for the extension of the chapel by one short bay, which would house the organ. Above was a great rose window partly inspired by the rose in the transepts of Old St Paul's Cathedral. Westward of this was to be a semicircular antechapel with an octagonal vault. This was to rise to the height of the aisles, and be supported from within by a single central shaft. It would form a prelude to a view of the chapel seen through two massive arches that maintained the rhythm of the arcades. The school buildings were to be attached to the antechapel by another great arch. The scale of the building made an apparently small extension an expensive undertaking.

In 1957, work was begun on finishing the antechapel by the addition of the corner pinnacles. Extensive work was done to make new foundations. Construction advanced, with the results becoming visible from 1961 onwards. The north-west staircase reached the upper chapel level, and in 1962 the cloister was linked to the porch. From 1964 to 1968, the pulpitum was completed and the south-west corner built up to the level of the aisles. However, the extension was far from finished at the time of its projected date of completion. Inflation caused a steep rise in costs, yet the Friends were not discouraged. Handford maintained their momentum: 'With God's blessing and renewed human effort, within a few years now Lancing Chapel may be complete, perhaps the last great Gothic building that will ever be built.'

In 1972, designs for the rose window and the heraldic stained glass were made and a fresh appeal launched. Dykes Bower proposed a window symbolising the unity of the schools of the Woodard Corporation in their central minster: 'The shield of Lancing is in the centre surrounded by the motto of the Corporation. The petals of the inner rose are filled with decorative ornament leading to the arms in the trefoils of the dioceses in which the schools are situated.' It was an ingenious arrangement, in which serendipitously the number of schools and dioceses helped to govern the design. A. E. Buss, of Goddard and Gibbs Studios, executed the glass under Dykes Bower's supervision.[11]

As the building was completed so it was improved, furnished and decorated under a comprehensive approach. Thousands of pounds were spent on research in order to achieve the right diffusion of light and eliminate halation. In 1977 as the narthex approached completion, the wood ceiling beneath the pulpitum was painted by Campbell Smith & Co. An exercise in the French geometrical Gothic of the thirteenth century, it was Dykes Bower's personal gift and is typical of his controlled polychromatic decoration. It counteracted the relatively subdued light of the narthex and made the first view of the chapel itself more dramatic. New stalls, executed by W. Mabbett & Sons, matched the canopies of the existing stalls, originally in Eton Chapel, and were returned on each side of the narthex; a canopy was added to the pulpit as a final unifying element.

Dykes Bower had an aversion to over-lit churches and disliked floodlighting. Comper's solution of grouping clear bulbs in gilded balls suspended from chandeliers was adapted for Lancing. Long pendants made of iron chains broken by gilded orbs were suspended from the centre of each bay at the level of the triforium. They terminate in a hoop of inverted scrolls, influenced by J. F. Bentley's lighting fittings in Westminster Cathedral, decorated with gilded pyramids at their intersections, from which are depended 20 bulbs in gilded balls. The illumination spread over the stall canopies onto the nave and into the aisles without disturbing the scale. Architecturally conceived, the black-and-gold wrought iron, executed by Furneaux, complements the stone and in its delicacy acts as a foil to the furniture.

On 13 May 1978 the Archbishop of Canterbury, Dr Coggan, in the presence of the Prince of Wales, consecrated the rose window and west wall. However, despite misleading press statements the chapel would not be finished until the antechapel was built, and Dykes Bower took every opportunity to make it clear that the blocked western arches were only temporary.[12] In 1981, new hangings and altar frontals improved the chapels at the east ends of the aisles, and he designed a window for the Lady Chapel in the north aisle. This was composed of lozenges set in grisaille on the theme of those who had built the chapel.

These were, however, minor consolations, and with press attention focused on the sheer size of the window he wrote to Handford:

The rose window and its glass ought not to distract attention from the real work of 20 years which, perhaps because of this length of time, is perhaps – in its magnitude – not realised by those whose memory does not go back as far. The window is only one part of the total design; but an impression could easily be created that its glass is what is to be dedicated and that the window was already there.[13]

Dykes Bower planned for two organ chambers to the north and south and a divided organ like those at Westminster Abbey and Liverpool, but in 1980 a move was made to build a new organ to go onto the pulpitum in a central position. This would be an architectural blunder, destroying the view through the west arches from the antechapel to the chapel and vice versa. It would also be wrong tonally, because the organ would be 'speaking' eastwards into the chapel whereas to be effective it should be placed in the antechapel itself. The proposal was the opening salvo in a long battle conducted

above: Lancing College Chapel, the rose window

by the music department of the college against the Friends and Dykes Bower, who as a musician disliked the prevailing fashion for baroque organs and was implacably opposed to the modification of his design.

Pressure for the organ intensified, and the need for a new campaign of stone restoration made Lancing decide to dismiss Dykes Bower. Alan Rome was appointed to design and supervise the organ project and to ensure that the stone restoration should not have an adverse effect upon it. Dykes Bower took it badly and was never reconciled to the overassertive central organ with its coarse detail and sentimental menagerie of animals in the carving. It was the first serious misjudgement in the furnishing of Lancing Chapel. While it remains it will discourage the completion of the chapel to Dykes Bower's design, by making nonsense of the spatial articulation and rendering the function of the antechapel meaningless.[14]

Until the debacle of the organ, Lancing had displayed high aesthetic standards of taste and workmanship. The chapel remains a potent symbol of conservative nineteenth- and twentieth-century Anglican taste. Handford composed a Latin inscription which makes plain that Dykes Bower's work still awaits completion: *Ad majoram dei gloriam et in honoram architecti Stephani Dykes Bower qui per XXX annos hanc aedem adeo imperfectum insigni perficiebat.* [To the greater glory of God and the honour of Stephen Dykes Bower who for 30 years worked on this still unfinished edifice.]

Later Church Designs

In contrast to the sad end to Dykes Bower's work at Lancing, Felsted School Chapel provided one of the happiest associations of this period. Between 1962 and 1964, he enlarged F. Chancellor's chapel of 1873 with new east and west ends and a new flèche. Furnishing included the colouring of the organ case and the glazing of the apse windows with fragmentation glass. The work continued until 1983, with the furnishing of a side chapel in memory of J. K. Bickerstaff, Headmaster of Felsted from 1933 to 1943.

In a corner of Dykes Bower's office at Quendon lay a heap of rolls of finished drawings. Attached to them was a note written in unusually strident terms, 'These were put aside on the instigation of G. G. Pace who, without a word to me, submitted a design of his own so bad that I declined to be associated with any cathedral that accepted such rubbish. His design was subsequently rejected and the work given to A. Bailey.'[15] They had consumed a great deal of time in the office and constituted a major project.

The Diocese of Sheffield was created in 1914, and Sir Charles Nicholson, a baronet, a pupil of J. D. Sedding and an architect of the Arts and Crafts Movement, made plans for a new cathedral. These were stalled by the war and Depression, and after Nicholson's death in 1949 Dykes Bower was appointed in his place. He prepared two finished designs in line with Nicholson's scheme but less ambitious, embodying the scholarly, literate ideals of twentieth-century traditional English church architecture. One proposal was in the Early English style of Gothic architecture, and this was the first time the style had been proposed for a modern church since the death of J. L. Pearson in 1897. Although

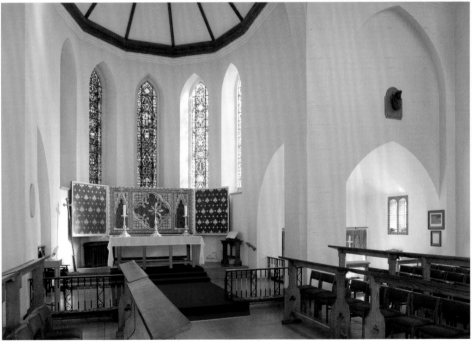

top: Felsted School Chapel, Essex, 1962–64, with Dykes Bower's addition in the foreground
above: Felsted School Chapel, refurnishing of the high altar

Eric Milner-White, Dean of York and the principal arbiter of taste in the Church of England, warmly approved of them, he suggested that George Pace, a young, promising, but untested, local architect should be appointed joint architect. It did not take long for Pace to gain the confidence of the Dean and Chapter and abandon the historical approach to architecture. Despite the beauty and scholarship of Dykes Bower's designs, in 1955 the Dean and Chapter were persuaded to accept Pace's radically different proposals. These, in turn, were abandoned, and in 1961 Pace submitted fees of £33,000, a practice never applied by Dykes Bower when schemes fell by the wayside. Milner-White later regretted his patronage of Pace, and Dykes Bower would delight in recalling that his last words were, 'Keep Pace out of the Minster.'

If one of Dykes's Bower's proposals had been executed it would have thrown St Edmundsbury into the shade. This incident at Sheffield not only demonstrated a major shift of Anglican church taste, of equal significance as the battle between Sir Giles Gilbert Scott and Sir Basil Spence at Coventry, but also the rejection of traditional church design of the most accomplished artistry.

The Sheffield story demonstrates the shifting background to church architecture in the 1960s. In addition to Pace, Lawrence King and Bernard Feilden emerged as rivals to Dykes Bower as Modernism began to affect cathedral and church architecture. Many of the younger clergy were tired of official Anglican taste and each of these younger architects appealed to a more progressive mood, while retaining enough traditional elements to gain the support of conservatives.

The Central Council for the Care of Churches had, some thought, become hidebound, and John Piper, the painter, was one of the first to challenge its supremacy in 1944 when he mounted a travelling exhibition for the Council for the Encouragement of Music and the Arts, 'The Artist and the Church'. He accused the Central Council of being rooted in the late nineteenth century and of having 'separated itself finally from the main and most vital roots of this country to become, on the whole, etiolated, provincial and over-traditional.' Thirteen years later, in 1957, Peter Hammond gave a talk on the Third Programme wireless station, 'Contemporary Architecture and the Church', in which he criticised what he considered to be the timidity and retrogression of contemporary English church architecture: 'Everywhere we find the same uncritical acceptance of late-medieval tradition, the same nostalgic regard for the Middle Ages as the Christian era *par excellence*.'[16]

This was not only a discussion about style, however. The burgeoning influence of the Continental liturgical movement emphasised the centralised eucharistic space, radically changing settled church planning. Theologically, the national Church was moving towards Liberal Protestantism. These influences contributed further towards Dykes Bower's isolation.

Dykes Bower was implicated in these criticisms, yet through its intelligence and sensitivity his work belongs in a different category. He was not directly influenced by the Continental liturgical movement, or by the early experiments that appeared in isolated English parishes after the Second World War. Bodies like the New Churches

Research Group were antipathetic to him, yet he was sympathetic to clergymen who were finding the remoteness of long chancels counterproductive to corporate worship.

The Parish Communion movement made the Eucharist, followed by the communal parish breakfast, its object and ideal; it was the principal liturgical force in the immediate post-war years, when congregations were largely composed of newly married, demobilised soldiers who missed the camaraderie of the forces. These ideas were brought to England shortly before the war by Fr Gabriel Hebert SSM, a monk of the Society of the Sacred Mission, Kelham, who was inspired by the Benedictine liturgical reforms of the Abbey of Marialaach in Germany. The movement emphasised the doctrine of the Church as the one family of God. It was a joining of entire families, gathered to offer the Holy Sacrifice in order that they may be made into one supernatural family in the Church.

Both Comper, who applied his developed liturgical plans from first principles that he had worked out for himself, and Dykes Bower, who was persuaded by him of the legitimacy of nave altars, avoided Hammond's accusations and responded to the needs of the time. Where necessary, Dykes Bower could design centrally planned sanctuaries with taste and success. The nave altar he installed in St Mary's, Bedford, in 1935 proved early on that a central altar need not be clumsy or obtrusive, but integral to the

above: Sheffield Cathedral extension with proposed new nave in brick, drawn by Alan Rome

above: Sheffield Cathedral, interior perspective of proposed extension in stone, drawn by Alan Rome, 1956

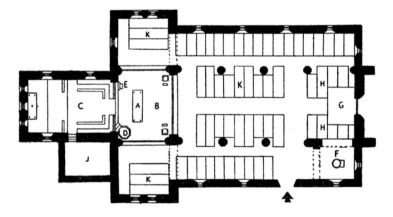

top: St Elvan's, Aberdare, Glamorgan. Scheme for nave altar, drawn by Hugh Mathew, 1968
above: The reshaping of St Paul's, Charleston, Cornwall, 1951

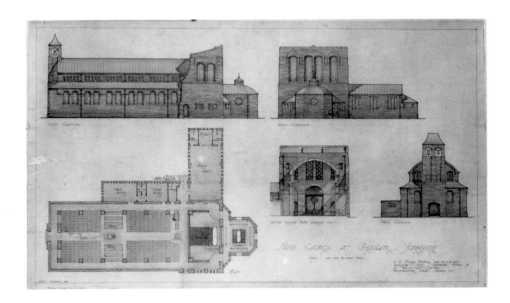

setting. Hammond's book, *Liturgy and Architecture*, published in 1960, illustrated with approval, Dykes Bower's proposal for replanning the cruciform church at Charlestown, Cornwall ten years previously. Hammond's work encouraged the foundation of groups that saw an absolute equivalence between liturgical reform and Modernist architecture, and, in Dykes Bower's despairing view, the result was the ruination of many English churches and the building of feeble modern ones of little lasting value that are unlikely to keep their centenaries.

Single-mindedly, Dykes Bower continued his work as inspecting architect to English cathedrals – Norwich, Ely, Carlisle, Gloucester, Exeter, Chelmsford, Wells and Christ Church Oxford – and to 150 parish churches. In all his work, Dykes Bower maintained the best Anglican standards. Regrettably, some of it, notably at Oxford and Chelmsford, has since ruthlessly been swept away.

St John the Baptist, Newcastle-upon-Tyne, replanned by Dykes Bower, is a big, late-medieval parish church which had been furnished by Nicholson and which also had a seventeenth-century Gothic font cover of the Bishop Cosin school of woodcarving. Alan Carefull, the vicar, was a conservative Anglo-Catholic and a man of means. He followed the modern liturgical reforms but did not want St John's to be barbarised. As a former curate of St John's, Tue Brook, he was deeply impressed by Dykes Bower's work, but uncertain whether he would be willing to design a new sanctuary at the crossing of the nave and transepts. The present writer persuaded him that Dykes Bower was not simply a decorator but would be able to design it in a way that would not spoil the building.

above: **Proposed new church at Redcar, first scheme, 1960**

Dykes Bower believed that in a transeptal church like St John's, a nave altar 'must not downgrade the altar in the chancel which has been there since the church was built by making it look as if it no longer had a purpose and was superfluous. ... The altar must always be worthy of its place and purpose in a church.'[17] Nicholson's long, low Gothic altar was recoloured in 1969, and later the chancel was turned into a chapel. Between 1971 and 1976, the rest of the church was improved. A light screen of wrought iron, painted black and gold and executed by Eric Stephenson, was thrown across the chancel to provide a background to the new ritual enclosure. Apart from a garish modern carpet laid by Carefull's successor without Dykes Bower's advice, St John's became an exemplary illustration of how a church should be replanned in a way that served the reformed liturgy and helped the building to express itself by making its significance fuller and clearer.

Only once did Dykes Bower design a church on a purely central plan. This was for a new parish in South Redcar, in the North Riding of Yorkshire, following his churches at Middlesbrough and Cambridge. Two designs were made, both for brick structures. The first was on a basilican plan with the altar at the east end and a Lady Chapel placed beyond. The second, drawn in 1965, was dramatically different. It was made on a square

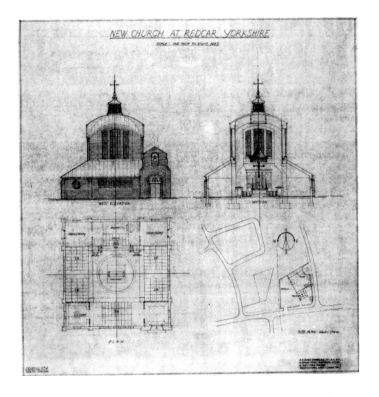

above: Proposed new church at Redcar, revised scheme with central altar, 1965

above: St John's, Newcastle, new nave altar and screen, 1968–76. This was Dykes Bower's last major re-planning scheme

Greek cross plan with the altar, surrounded by circular communion rails and blocks of seats, standing at the centre beneath a large lantern which provided the main source of light. Vestries, baptistery and porch were contained in the corners, and he proposed that the altar would stand beneath a suspended Classical tester made of red silk. The designs were rejected in 1967. Had this church been built it would have been one of the most progressive, as far as planning was concerned, in the country. Its beautiful interior might have established a benchmark for liturgical design conceived in traditional terms. Neither design was realised, and thereafter Dykes Bower was offered no more opportunities for building new churches.

Notes

1   *Architects' Journal*, 20 April 1983, pp.40–3. *Brick Builder*, March 1959, p.563; December 1959, p.9.
2   Geoffrey Tyack, Simon Bradley and Nikolaus Pevsner, *The Buildings of England: Berkshire, London and New Haven*, Yale University Press, 2010, p.394.
3   Nikolaus Pevsner, *The Buildings of England: Cambridge,* Harmondsorth, Penguin Books, 1970, p.253; Nicholas Taylor and Philip Booth, *Cambridge New Architecture*, 3rd edition, London, Leonard Hill Books, 1970, p.120.
4   *The Times*, 8 May 1961, p.14.
5   *The Times*, 2 July 1970, p.8.
6   Nikolaus Pevsner, *The Buildings of England: Norfolk*, Harmondsworth, Penguin Books, 1976, p.145.
7   Nikolaus Pevsner, *The Buildings of England: Sussex*, Harmondsworth, Penguin Books, 1965, p.258.
8   *The Times,* 10 June 1952, p.7; *Lancing College Magazine*, vol. 48-1, no. 500, Lent 1955. This edition of the magazine was devoted to the history of the chapel and to promoting Dykes Bower's scheme. I am grateful to the Revd John Hunwicke for assembling a file of correspondence and references to Dykes Bower's work at Lancing.
9   Canon Adam Fox, *Lancing College Magazine, op. cit.*
10 Letter from Stephen Dykes Bower to Basil Handford, 18 October 1971, Lancing College archives.
11 *The Times*, 14 October 1976, p.4.
12 ibid.
13 Letter from Stephen Dykes Bower to Basil Handford, 20 October 1976, Lancing College archives.
14 Letter from Stephen Dykes Bower to the headmaster, 24 July 1980, setting out his objections to the new organ; *Lancing College Magazine*, vol. 76-5, no. 578, December 1986, Lancing College archives.
15 I am grateful to Warwick Pethers for drawing my attention to this note, and to Alan Powers for providing me with a copy.
16 Peter Hammond, 'Contemporary Architecture and the Church', *Listener*, 21 November 1957, p.839. This subject is discussed in the chapter 'John Betjeman, John Piper and Sir Ninian Comper: *Of the Atmosphere of a Church* in Context' in Anthony Symondson and Stephen Bucknall, *Sir Ninian Comper: An introduction to his life and work with complete gazetteer*, Reading, Ecclesiological Society and Spire Books, 2006, pp.206–30.
17 Stephen Dykes Bower to Anthony Symondson, 15 September 1970.

6   Restoration: Painted Decoration and Church Interiors

Painted Churches

Perhaps the most fragile legacy of Victorian architecture is the painted church interior. A. W. N. Pugin had revived polychromatic painted decoration on the walls of churches in stiff, diapered patterns executed in heraldic colour. The painted interior reached the highest point of perfection in the work of G. F. Bodley, who employed Morris, Marshall, Faulkner & Co. for this task in some of his early churches – notably SS Michael and All Angels', Brighton, and St Martin's, Scarborough – and Frederick Leach of Cambridge thereafter.

At Queens' College, Cambridge in 1875, Bodley made an outstanding restoration of the fifteenth-century timber roof of the hall and decorated the walls in flowing diaper patterns in tones of green. In 1891, he built the chapel, whose east wall, reredos, ceiling and organ case were decorated in tones of red and black brightened with gilding, but by 1952 the work was faded. Dykes Bower recognised the inherent qualities of Bodley's work, and, acting under his direction, Queens' clerk of works faithfully repainted the hall and chapel to the original colours and tones. New hangings in Bodley's Pine Tapestry that had been especially rewoven by Watts & Co. completed the work in the chapel. For its time, the restoration was unique for the extent to which Bodley's work was taken seriously and accepted on its own terms.

This led in 1960 to the restoration work for Sir George Gilbert Scott's magnificently decorated roof timbers in the Great Hall of St John's College, Cambridge, undertaken under Dykes Bower's direction by Campbell Smith & Co. In the same context, the roof of Carlisle Cathedral, designed by Owen Jones in 1860, was another major scheme restored by Dykes Bower and executed by the same firm during his time as Consultant to the Fabric. It was turned into a firmament of blue and gold, and the tone was dependent upon J. N. Comper's application of Mediterranean colour while faithfully keeping to Jones's pattern.

Northern Church Commissions

The restoration in 1967 of Bodley's church of St John, Tue Brook, Liverpool, the last church designed by Bodley before he entered into partnership with Thomas Garner in 1868, marked a significant development in the treatment of painted Victorian church

opposite: The hall of Queens' College, Cambridge, mid-15th century, restoration by G. F. Bodley with Morris & Co., repainted to the original colours by Dykes Bower, 1967

decoration. It was the first fully developed late-Victorian parish church in England, and anticipated the flowering of the Gothic Revival in late-Gothic terms. Charles Eastlake singled out St John's for praise in *A History of the Gothic Revival*, recognising the 'charm of colour' and an 'additional element of beauty which pervades the whole building from its primary construction to the last touch of its embellishment.'[1]

At St John's, Tue Brook, Bodley had effaced some murals by C. E. Kempe, originally commissioned in the clerestory, and replaced them with patterns; St John's remained, perhaps, the best and most complete painted church interior of the time. By the 1960s, it reminded Peter Anson of a 'much worn Persian carpet'.[2] Many saw beauty in the faded hues, but parts of the decoration had badly deteriorated and the point came at which restoration was necessary. Canon Frank Samson, the vicar, invited Lawrence King to prepare a plan and he recommended a loud scheme of selective colouring. The author was involved in the sequence of events that led to Dykes Bower's employment instead. His approach to St John's was then quite novel. He recognised, as he had at Queens', the integral value and beauty of Bodley's scheme and wanted to return it to the original freshness. This involved the careful copying of many of the patterns on the ceilings and walls, but he left Kempe's surviving murals alone and simply cleaned them.

St John's saw a development of Dykes Bower's move to preserve discarded, less fashionable Victorian church furniture from the later decades of the nineteenth century, including Bodley's altar screen of 1882 that covered the east wall of Dunstable Priory. This was removed 90 years later and faced destruction until Dykes Bower found a place for it against the west wall beneath the tower of St John's, where it quickly looked as if it was meant to be there. He also designed some simple oak furniture that was equally congruous.

The work was finished in 1976, a year after it had won an Award of Exceptional Merit during European Architectural Heritage Year. So successful was the restoration (despite being left incomplete) that it opened a new understanding of how Victorian painted church interiors should be preserved, and has had consequences as far-reaching as Bodley's own work.

The immediate after-effect of St John's, Tue Brook, was the restoration in 1971–9 of the interior of St Augustine's, Pendlebury, Manchester (1871–4), Bodley & Garner's early masterpiece and perhaps the greatest church of the late Gothic Revival, if not of the whole movement. Seeing St Augustine's for the first time, Dykes Bower wrote, 'No church has thrilled me more and the glass is *superlatively* beautiful.'[3] Never as fortunate in legacies and a well-to-do congregation as St John's, Pendlebury had a decaying parish with a poor urban congregation. But grants were obtained and the Revd Frank Brown, the elderly vicar, started a courageous fundraising drive. These enabled the ceiling and chancel walls to be repainted, the broken furniture repaired, the glass restored by Dennis King, and the unsatisfactory heating system to be removed, but it was

opposite: Queens' College chapel, architect G F Bodley, 1890–1, with painted decoration restored by Dykes Bower, 1952. East window by C.E. Kempe, side widows by John Hardman & Co

above: St John's, Tue Brook, Liverpool, architect G F Bodley, 1868, painted decoration reconstructed by Dykes Bower, 1967

top: St John's, Tue Brook, detail of painted roof
above: St John's, Tue Brook, looking west

impossible to bring the church to the standard of perfection which Dykes Bower desired. It became harder to raise funds and the work slowed down. Dykes Bower commented:

> *So far restoration, for lack of money, has got no further than the west wall but I hope the reredos will show people how marvellous the whole building could be if everything, including the wall diapers (still existing under the whitewash) were restored in full. It maddens one to see the ignorant way in which past clerics treated churches of this calibre, but I think I have now got evidence to prove Bodley's intentions for almost every part of it.[4]*

What was accomplished moved St Augustine's on to a new footing with much of its original splendour regained.

The restoration of the interior of St Salvador's, Dundee (1868–74), an early church by Bodley, was accomplished by the painting conservator, Rab Snowden, directed by the architectural historian, Colin McWilliam, and the Scottish Georgian Society. Walpamur, a paint manufacturer, had approached the rector and suggested a scheme which would apply a different pastel colour to each wall, lightening and brightening, it was thought, a dark interior. McWilliam had heard from the author of Dykes Bower's work in Liverpool and went to see it. Although St Salvador's could not then afford to

above: St Augustine, Pendlebury, architect G F Bodley, 1871–4

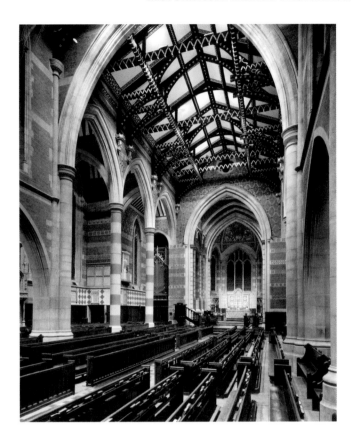

use Dykes Bower, he went there in 1971 and saw his work bearing fruit, if in a more conservative spirit, such that he had to be restrained from trying to touch up Burlison & Grylls's tympanum above the reredos when he was inspecting it on the scaffold.[5] This was an early example of Dykes Bower's influence on other specialists in the field, and remains one of the most impressive.

Decoration and Restoration

Dykes Bower should not exclusively be associated with the late Gothic Revival. He admired the perfect example of unity and form achieved by William Burges, especially at St Finn Barr's Cathedral, Cork (1862–79). He also admired, with qualifications, the work of William Butterfield, and in 1960, before the restorations at St John's, Tue Brook, and St Augustine's, Pendlebury, he had renewed the geometrical painted decoration in the chapel ceiling at Rugby School (1870–72), turning the reredos into a triptych decorated in bold patterns taken from Butterfield's constructional polychromy.

above: Rugby School Chapel, architect William Butterfield, 1870–2, redecorated by Dykes Bower, 1958–61

Nowadays, in an age of careful and austere conservation, Dykes Bower's approach in which entire sections of pattern and colour were repainted would be frowned upon, but few then thought seriously of retaining the original painted surfaces of nineteenth-century and later work. With Bodley, Dykes Bower remained faithful to the master's subtle half tones, demonstrating that the Victorian painted church interior was valuable in itself and also capable of restoration. The balance of taste has changed, and few now consider that an existing scheme should not be treated in terms of its integrity. As a result, some obliterated schemes have been reinstated and faded work conserved.

Holy Spirit and St Alban, Portsmouth

Of all the churches of the Gothic Revival, the one that Dykes Bower most admired was George Gilbert Scott Junior's masterpiece, St Agnes', Kennington Park, London (1874–91) – the noblest and most beautiful church of the late Gothic Revival. In 1941, its roof was destroyed by fire but the walls and fine furniture survived. T. Francis Bumpus, the ecclesiologist, believed:

> with its magnificent screens, stained glass, altar pieces, roof paintings, graceful
> arcades and ample chair-seated area, [it] might be taken for a church built
> during the palmiest days of the Early Perpendicular period by some wealthy
> wool-stapler who had brought with him reminiscences of Flanders.[6]

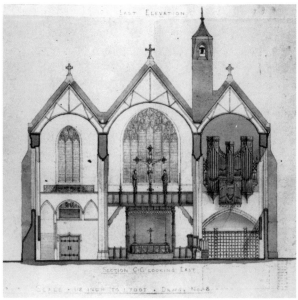

above:　Left, St. Agnes, Kennington (1874–91), by George Gilbert Scott Jnr. Right, The Holy Spirit, Southsea, cross section of a roof beam a version simply showing the proposed rood beam, loft and figures from St Agnes', Kennington, organ and other furnishings

The Council for the Care of Churches informed the War Damage Commissioners that, 'we feel that this church may be considered the most important 19th century building to have been damaged in the last war, and we suggest that it needs special treatment'.

In 1946, Dykes Bower was appointed the architect charged with the church's restoration, reporting that what survived represented 75 per cent of the cost of rebuilding. The War Damage Commission agreed to pay for full restitution but, scandalously, the Diocese of Southwark used the money to demolish the building and replaced it with a humble substitute that contained only a little of the surviving furniture.[7]

St Matthew's, Southsea, Portsmouth, was built of red brick by J. T. Micklethwaite and finished, after his death in 1906, by Sir Charles Nicholson. It was one of the most refined of Micklethwaite's churches, notable for its aspiring height, careful detail and scale, with the aisles of the same height as the nave. At the east end of the north aisle is an elevated Lady Chapel approached by a flight of steps. The tall arcades, which rise to the ceiling, were originally finished with moulded capitals. St Matthew's was bombed during the Second World War and the parish combined with St Bartholomew's, Southsea, when the united parish was rededicated to the Holy Spirit. Dykes Bower was appointed as architect for the restoration.

Once again, his desire to preserve good furniture from closed and destroyed churches gave him an opportunity to find a home in the Holy Spirit for the significant body of undamaged furniture surviving at St Agnes', Kennington – a good solution to a serious problem, as there were few churches big enough to take it. Architecturally, the church was a conspicuous example of the bare style, dependent stylistically on St Agnes' for its own scale, materials and detail, reinforced by a further debt, created by the absence of a clerestory, to St Mary Magdalene's, Munster Square, London, by R. C. Carpenter, where Micklethwaite himself worshipped until his death.

Dykes Bower decided to remould the arcades at Holy Spirit by removing the capitals and replaced them with arches dying in their piers as they were at St Agnes', going far towards replicating the setting for the furniture. Above all, he wanted to re-erect the rood, screen and loft, but, although these elements were brought to the church and put in store, this was deemed too expensive. The font and cover, by Temple Moore, and the pulpit were put in place, and much of the surviving glass by Kempe was adapted for the east windows. The returned stalls from the screen were kept along with minor pieces of furniture, but the incomplete project fell short of the opportunity to create one of the best church interiors in the country and pay full tribute to George Gilbert Scott Junior's genius.

In addition, Dykes Bower designed a Gothic ciborium magnum, or baldacchino, to cover the high altar, and an organ case – but these, also, were too expensive to execute. A long altar, furnished with tall, silver ornaments made by Frank Knight, stood at the east end beneath a dorsal of rich tapestry. Even in its partly furnished form, the Holy Spirit was one of the best, most sensitive, ethereal and dignified, post-war church restorations in the UK.

Dykes Bower's association with the building continued until the 1980s, the interior surviving unspoilt in its austere, almost Cistercian, perfection until 2009, when radical changes were made. Dykes Bower's high altar was replaced by a small, square altar of limestone and moved to a chapel in the south aisle. Temple Moore's pulpit was superseded by a new limestone ambo, and his font and cover by the new font; these were returned to the rebuilt St Agnes', Kennington. All that survives of Dykes Bower's work are four of the six silver candlesticks, placed at each corner of the new altar.

No replanning of the Holy Spirit could have been more abrasive in its modernity and liturgical naivety or less sympathetic to a building characterised by taste, learning, refinement, and restraint. Of all Dykes Bower's distinguished post-war restorations, this is the one that has suffered most from brutally insensitive and unnecessary alteration.

St Alban, Copnor, Portsmouth, was designed by Sir Charles Nicholson and built in 1913–14. It had an English liturgical tradition and, unlike many churches of this date, it was completely furnished in a synthesis of late-Gothic and Jacobean styles. The church was bombed in 1941 and the west end destroyed. In 1961, Dykes Bower was commissioned to rebuild it by the Revd Richard Corbet-Milward, a cultivated man of means, and embarked on an extensive scheme of decoration, furnishing and replanning. Work started in 1963 and during the next nine years the walls were whitened; the roofs, rood and pulpit recoloured; and the high altar reredos restored.

above: **The Holy Spirit, Southsea, the Dykes Bower scheme as existing until 2009**

A nave altar was required, demanding major changes. Nicholson's Jacobean chancel screen was removed to the west end of the nave to form a narthex and baptistery. A new screen in the Renaissance style replaced it, before which was placed a long altar raised on a shallow predella, and the chancel was turned into a chapel. Dykes Bower designed a painted font cover and applied further colour in the form of figured hangings and vestments of silk, those in the Lady Chapel embroidered by Winifrid Peppiatt. The result is one of the most exquisitely furnished modern churches in southern England, glowing with colour. Few others embody so fully the principles and ideals of pre-First World War aspirations continuing until the second half of the twentieth century.

St Paul's and Christ Church, Manchester

The early 1970s began to see the dispersal on an extensive scale of church furniture, caused by the implementation of the liturgical reforms of the Second Vatican Council. Echoes were increasingly to be found in the Church of England but a stronger impulse came from the Pastoral Measure, 1968, which has led since 1969 to the closure of over 1,500 churches, among them many, from all periods, of serious architectural distinction. Nineteenth-century town churches of the Gothic Revival were the most frequent victims. Too many had been built, and slum clearance and demographic change made

above: The Holy Spirit, Southsea, cross and candlesticks designed by Dykes Bower and made by Frank Knight

many redundant. Frequently they had good stained glass and furniture that deserved a better future than architectural salvage. It was in this climate that Dykes Bower achieved some of the best results in his later work.

Two churches, both in Manchester, were transformed in this way and saved from an uncertain future: St Paul's, Paddington, Salford, built by E. H. Shellard in 1856, and Christ Church, Moss Side, built by W. Cecil Hardisty in 1904. Both had remarkable parish priests who wanted their bare, poorly furnished churches to appeal more attractively to their congregations.

When Canon David Wyatt was appointed to St Paul's, Salford, in 1968, he found the church derelict and awaiting demolition in the centre of a housing estate of monumental point blocks. A new church in the Modernist style was planned, but Wyatt saw that the old building was a powerful symbol of continuity and hope, as a modern substitute never would be. He had come to know Dykes Bower's work when he was an undergraduate at Cambridge. Dykes Bower designed a new vicarage with a parish hall, cloister and garden providing an oasis in a desert of concrete that has come to be greatly valued by those who live around it. The traditional style of the new buildings was strongly opposed by the planning authority but this was overcome and, on completion, the slate-hung cloister was once mistaken for the work of Temple Moore.[8]

St Paul's has little architectural interest, but follows the spirit of Pugin and Sir George Gilbert Scott. Dykes Bower saw that the proportions and simplicity of its design would make a good setting for church furniture. Before adding new pieces, he drew out the better qualities of the shell by painting the roof and whitening the walls. Wyatt wanted a nave altar, and this was put against a light screen of wrought iron in which Norman Furneaux incorporated discarded work from Chelmsford Cathedral; it opened onto the splendidly furnished high altar.

Furniture was acquired over many years from demolished Manchester churches and seamlessly incorporated. Arts and Crafts choir stalls and pews were brought from St Anne's, Brindle Heath; a robust, square marble font, heavily carved, from St Alban's, Rochdale; and a delicate calvary from St Gabriel's, Hulme. The royal arms came from Christ Church, Salford, and a late eighteenth-century organ case from St Thomas's, Ardwick. Yet all look perfectly congruous and the work of a controlling mind. Dykes Bower admired Canon Wyatt, saw his difficulties and rarely charged fees.

Christ Church, Moss Side (1899–1904), is, in contrast, a lofty, graceful church of red brick by a local architect, W. Cecil Hardisty, who was influenced by Bodley and George Gilbert Scott Junior, that had never been properly furnished owing to the First World War. Christ Church, serving a similar parish to St Paul's and surrounded by an estate of point blocks, was bound for redundancy when the Revd Harry Ogden was appointed in 1970.

opposite: St Alban's, Copnor, Portsmouth, architect Sir Charles Nicholson, 1913–4, rebuilt and furnished by Dykes Bower after bomb damage, 1963–72

top: The cloister garden at St Paul's, Salford, with the vicarage and parish hall, 1968 onwards
above left: Canon David Wyatt at St Paul the Apostle, Salford, with Dykes Bower's gates made from salvaged ventilation grilles behind
above right: St Paul's, Salford, architect Edwin H. Shellard, 1856, the refurnished and decorated interior

One of the noblest churches to be demolished under the Pastoral Measure was St Edward's, Holbeck, Leeds (1903–5), one of Bodley's last works. Its massive altar screen, carved and coloured, which covered the east wall was re-erected in Christ Church in 1981, in a new position at the top of an elevated chancel where awesomely it commands the church like a great Hispano-Flemish retable.

At Christ Church, Dykes Bower applied a less eclectic approach than at St Paul's. Late-Gothic furniture was retrieved to suit Hardisty's architecture, notably an organ case by John Oldrid Scott from St Peter's, Northampton; a font cover by Walter Tapper from St Erkenwald's, Southend; and a reredos by J. Harold Gibbons, a pupil of Temple Moore, for one of the chapels. In this way, two architecturally undistinguished churches were enriched and given new life in contemporary contexts. Dykes Bower continued to design new work and incorporate old in both until shortly before his death. One of his last works was an aumbry for Christ Church, designed in 1987.

top: The organ at Christ Church, Moss Side, designed by John Oldrid Scott for St Peter's, Northampton, redecorated by Dykes Bower
above: Dykes Bower's design for an aumbry at Christ Church Moss Side, his last executed work at the age of 84

Not all welcomed these developments. Canon Wilkinson, of Solihull, published a letter in *The Times* on 29 May 1981 illogically asserting that 'clergy who look after their churches thereby neglect to talk about God to their people'. Fr Ogden replied, 'My experience from observation of other parishes as well as my own is that the care and enhancement of "Victorian Gothic edifices" goes hand in hand with a renewal of spiritual life and the evangelistic outreach in inner-city parishes, decayed or otherwise.' He went on to praise Canon Wyatt for saving St Paul's, Salford, and putting it under the 'sensitive guidance' of Dykes Bower, declaring that this was the 'main instrument in

above: Christ Church, Moss Side, architect W. Cecil Hardisty, 1899–1904, the interior refurnished by Dykes Bower with the reredos by G. F. Bodley from St Edward, Holbeck, Leeds, and other salvaged items

top: Carlisle Cathedral, Memorial Chapel of the King's Own Royal Border Regiment, 1949
above: Drawing for the Border Regiment chapel screen

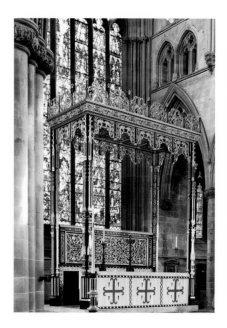 

turning a small aged congregation into the largest and most vigorous and most evange-listically effective congregation in the whole of Salford'. He concluded:

> *What better example could we follow, in inner-city areas and elsewhere?*
> *For the restoration, reordering and beautifying of old recognisable church*
> *buildings is an outward and visible sign which ordinary unsophisticated*
> *people immediately recognise – that neither God nor his Church are dead,*
> *and that he is quite capable of making new that which had grown old, and*
> *of lifting up that which had fallen down.*[9]

Carlisle Cathedral

For 40 years (1948–88) Dykes Bower was consultant architect to Carlisle Cathedral, the least spoilt of all the medieval cathedrals with which he was associated and most complete in terms of what he added. Sir Charles Nicholson, his predecessor, furnished the chapels of the choir aisles, and in 1934 had designed a ciborium magnum, or baldac-chino, and high altar in the English Renaissance style, taking hints from a surviving sixteenth-century screen in the choir and providing sound foundations for what came later.

First was the memorial chapel to the Border Regiment at the east end of the short nave, completed in 1949 and composed of a sanctuary formed from a bay enclosed

above left: Carlisle Cathedral, High Altar by Sir Charles Nicholson, redecorated by Dykes Bower in 1967
above right: Carlisle Cathedral, St Wilfrid's Chapel

within Classical screens of wrought iron, painted red and gold, that contained an altar with a pall frontal and tall Baroque ornaments made by Frank Knight. The ironwork was influenced by Tapper's work in York Minster and Comper's Spanish *rejas* (screens). One of the most successful examples of Dykes Bower's maturity, the chapel's orientation has recently been reversed to make way for a font but otherwise it remains the same. The redecoration of the ceilings and the recolouring and gilding of Nicholson's baldacchino and reredos followed in 1967. At the same time, a new cross and candlesticks were designed and a new pavement of Westmoreland slate laid in the sanctuary. The Flemish pulpit was restored and new stall fronts were provided for the congregational seating in the choir.

A surprising opportunity arose that enabled Dykes Bower to apply the same principles at Carlisle that he had achieved at Salford and Moss Side, occasioned by the return to Cumbria of an exquisite carved and gilded triptych of the Antwerp school, dating from *c*.1500. Formerly in the Broughton Chapel in Westmorland, it was set up in Carlisle, following conservation in 1971. This was followed by the acquisition of some stalls and an embroidered altar frontal of cut velvet designed by Bodley (both from different sources), and the work was harmoniously integrated and completed by a new Gothic screen of wrought iron, executed by Norman Furneaux, entirely different in character from those Dykes Bower had designed 20 years before in the regimental memorial chapel.

above: Carlisle Cathedral, painted ceiling of quire

Work at Quendon

From 1935 until his death, Dykes Bower restored and altered the modest parish church of St Simon and St Jude at Quendon, near Saffron Walden, removing various Victorian additions and installing new, clear-glazed windows with mullions and stout ferramenta. He removed the bellcote, substituting a wooden belfry in the Essex tradition, and restored the porch. Inside, he panelled the chancel, decorated the ceiling and provided a new reredos, ornaments and hangings for the high altar. Finally, he provided a new lectern and stalls and acted as churchwarden, treasurer, organist and choirmaster. He took his turn in dusting the church and tidying the churchyard. On the fiftieth anniversary of his appointment as organist, the choir gave him 1,000 daffodil bulbs and planted them in his meadow; it gave him enormous pleasure to see them naturalise. In 1962–5, he designed and built a new rectory. His work in Quendon church represented in miniature what he had achieved on a greater scale elsewhere, and has a delightful accretive quality in which everything looks as it should.

top: St Simon and St Jude's, Quendon, exterior with Dykes Bower's bellcote, 1965

Notes

1   Charles Locke Eastlake, *A History of the Gothic Revival*, London, Longmans, Green & Co., 1872, p.369.
2   Peter Anson, *Fashions in Church Furnishing*, London, Faith Press, 1960, p.230.
3   Stephen Dykes Bower to Anthony Symondson, 4 May 1970.
4   Stephen Dykes Bower to Anthony Symondson, 20 September 1978.
5   Conversation with the late Colin McWilliam.
6   T. Francis Bumpus, *London Churches Ancient and Modern*, 2nd Series, London, T. Werner Laurie, 1908, p.356.
7   Gavin Stamp, *Lost Victorian Britain: How the Twentieth Century Destroyed the Nineteenth Century's Architectural Masterpieces*, London, Aurum Press, 2010, pp.116–18.
8   *Salford City Reporter*, 29 June 1979.
9   *The Times*, 29 May 1981, p.13; and 5 June 1981, p.15.

above: Quendon Church, redecorated by Dykes Bower

TYPICAL PANE

AT BASE. (SEE
ACC

PAINT

PAINT

7   The Drawing Office

Before the Second World War, Dykes Bower worked entirely on his own, but after 1945 the volume of work became too much for him. In 1949, when he was working on the design for the new high altar of St Paul's Cathedral, W. Godfrey Allen, the Surveyor to the Fabric, introduced him to Reginald Kirby who became his first assistant, but he remained overstretched and still unable to afford more staff. Dykes Bower's influential supporter, William Croome, gave F. C. Eeles of the Central Council for the Care of Churches an account of his difficulties:

> As to his own position: that he has but one full-time Assistant (I think the man Kirby whom we met over the St Paul's model), who lives in Quendon and works all day in Quendon Court. That he has no typist or Secretary; and does all the original drawings with his own hand, Kirby copying them as necessary. Upon my urging that a man loaded with half-a-dozen cathedrals and the re-building of half-a-dozen of our largest destroyed churches could not possibly cope with his work unless better assisted, he replied that he was totally unable to afford anymore. That he is all the time running at a loss, and dependent upon his private income to make this good. That at the present time he works for months on Reports, Plans for re-building, future schemes like St Paul's, for all of which he receives barely out-of-pocket expenses ... He has had very little on account of St Paul's as yet; but says that if one of the bigger schemes like that got under way, he could begin to draw a steady income and could enlarge. It is a curious position; but it appears to be true. He says no scheme large enough to bring in adequate earnings ever gets a Licence; so he can earn little, though kept at a stretch with work and plans.[1]

It would have been physically impossible for Dykes Bower to work alone and do the detailed designing himself; yet he seldom referred to his associates. He had two drawing offices: one in his garden at Quendon Court, built in 1957–8, beneath a striking clock in a white cupola, the other at Westminster Abbey during his years as Surveyor. There were seldom more than two assistants, and three at most. Over the question of partnership with his colleagues, there was an element of concealment, since he argued that if he were seen to take a partner, it would be assumed he was no longer capable of running the practice. The appointment first of Reginald Kirby and later Hugh Mathew as *de facto* partners was necessary in order to retain them in the office, but their names were not added to the practice title, and Kirby's never appeared on the letterhead.

Kirby had been a member of the Modern Architectural Research Group (MARS), but

opposite: **Details from a design for an organ case for St. Mary's, Hayes, Middlesex, 1956**

became disenchanted with Modernism, suffering repudiation by many of his old friends. Hugh Mathew, a fine singer as well as architect, was given a letter of introduction to Dykes Bower by Dr Boris Ord of King's College, Cambridge, which he presented in 1957, having previously worked for Geoffrey Beech, the Diocesan Surveyor to Bath and Wells, and for W. J. Carpenter-Turner, the cathedral architect to Winchester. John O'Neilly, who previously worked for Sir Albert Richardson, had just left the Westminster Abbey drawing office, and Mathew's first work was to make full-size drawings for the flat ceiling over the crossing. Kirby died in 1966 while working on St Edmundsbury Cathedral and Mathew, who had been asked to work in the Quendon office, was employed continuously on Bury to the end of 1970. Dykes Bower entered into partnership with Mathew in 1969 and his name was added to the letterhead.

Alan Rome, a pupil of Sir George Oatley, was in the Westminster Abbey office in the 1950s. Pamela Hutchin worked at Quendon as a draughtswoman. Alfred Laycock, formerly chief assistant to Sir Edward Maufe, remained with Dykes Bower until he retired from the abbey in 1973. Warwick Pethers, who had taken courses at the

above left: Design for an organ case for Wimborne Minster.
above right: Design for monument to Bishop Headlam, Gloucester Cathedral

Architectural Association and the Regent Street Polytechnic, heard Dykes Bower give a lecture and was attracted by his defence of tradition. Dykes Bower responded to his interest by inviting him to lunch. They got on well and Dykes Bower offered to train Pethers in Gothic design, with the result that he spent the last years of Dykes Bower's career effectively working as in the manner of a Victorian articled pupil.

He not only learned Dykes Bower's methods but absorbed his way of thinking, seeing and general architectural knowledge. This enabled him later to complete St Edmundsbury Cathedral with complete conviction, while, on a personal level, Warwick and Susan Pethers did much for Dykes Bower's well-being and daily living as he grew older, sharing the house in his last two years and making his final years comfortable and happy. He was thus enabled to maintain his professional activity to the end.

Dykes Bower also used draughtsmen who worked for the contractors he employed. There were George Cockburn and Eric White of James Longley's, of Crawley; and W. F. Haslop, of Rattee and Kett, of Cambridge. Haslop has been described by Stephen Oliver as 'an intuitive designer and sculptor as well as a stonemason and careful restorer of buildings in his own right.' He worked closely with Dykes Bower on the restoration of Magdalene College, Cambridge, in 1950–66. This is a rare example of architect and

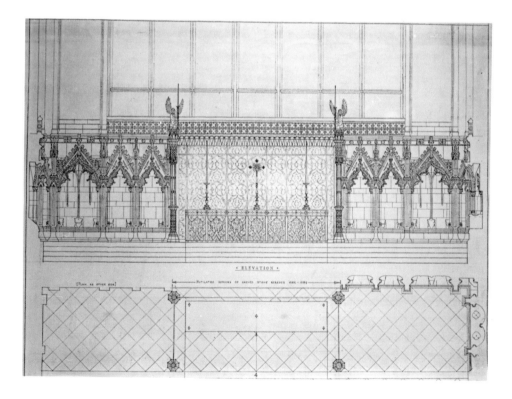

above: Design for furnishing the Lady Chapel, Ely Cathedral as the county war memorial, 1945, since destroyed

master builder working together, as Haslop's light-hearted letters to Dykes Bower suggest. Haslop's charming naive drawings are often annotated 'DB-WH' and his design for the riverfront chimneys is inscribed 'As agreed with Mr Dykes Bower MA, FRIBA, FSA 2.7.62. W. F. Haslop OBE, MA, FRSA … Take care of this drawing which took 1 hour plus 56 years.'[2] Haslop's qualifications were not part of the joke – all but the OBE were honorary but well deserved.

Dykes Bower ran the practice on late-Victorian lines, securing the work, exercising complete artistic control, attending site and committee meetings and, like A. W. N. Pugin and Sir George Gilbert Scott, travelling almost exclusively first class by train as he welcomed the opportunity for thought.

The early stages of a design were always worked out on a small scale. Take, for instance, the decoration of the ceiling of the abbey crossing. Mathew remembers 'enlarging in stages his tiny original designs for decoration of the first mahogany-boarded ceiling; adding and subtracting features, under his guidance, as it grew. Adjustments were made to scale and strength of colour, during the actual painting, from my full-size details: viewing from the crossing floor was made possible by the temporary removal of boards in the scaffold floor created for the painting.' Mathew regarded the small sketch made for this job as a remarkable example of Dykes Bower's methods. It contained, in essence,

above: St Paul's baldacchino, a cartoon possibly by W. F. Haslop

the entire design 'on a page torn from the little pocket-book he used for taking notes at meetings, on the back of which was one of the many Anglican chants he composed, for use by his choir of a few men and women in Quendon village church.'[3]

Rome remembered that this procedure was 'typical of DB's approach', explaining:

> *first small sketches and then from these an opportunity to develop a number of avenues (sometimes based on verbal suggestions alone). Again I was asked to make sketches for the Stratford-on-Avon Guild Chapel organ case and these were discussed, rejected, or adopted in part, corrected and vastly improved – often DB's method. This atelier atmosphere was great fun to work in, though sometimes with a deadline in the diary it was very hard work. The first set of drawings for St Nicholas', Great Yarmouth, fell into this category – all elevations and sections drawn and coloured in two weeks.*[4]
> *'Other designs', Rome remembered, '(those dearest to his heart) came down from Quendon fully worked out and drawn in minute detail. The Rugby School Chapel reredos wings and ornaments, all frontals, Abbey furnishings and memorials fell into this category. DB did not draw nearly as well as Oatley, and one had to work up building designs by stages ... Often a diminishing glass was used to view larger schemes – DB somehow found a small scale easier to control.*[5]
> *'In defence of his draughtsmanship,' Mathew believes, 'I must say that his small-scale designs for altar ornaments, say, were perfect in the delicacy of line and shape: every curve springing with life and vigour. Having to reproduce these designs to full size was to me a revelation of the subtleties of shape in the master's eye. Incidentally, a diminishing glass is a most valuable aid to any designer.*[6]

But these collaborative methods sometimes imposed strain on the assistants, especially when applied to major works. After Kirby's death, the east end of Wastell's nave at Bury St Edmunds had still to be structurally supported to allow the demolition of the east walls of the aisles and Scott's chancel arch. Excavations for deep foundations were needed for the tower and transepts that would join the old and new structures.

Mathew recalls, in detail, his having:

> *to design the western piers for the tower and completion of the eastern pair; the north and south tower arches, and the westernmost arch with its gallery in the thickness of the wall above for access from parapet level of the south transept with an open internal gallery over the south windows for access to the Lady Chapel parapets; the gallery in the thickness of the south transept gable for access to the eastern parapet; the three arches and stair to the future north transept over the cloister roof and the little stair down from the transept floor level to the cloister; and the tower walls carried up to the temporary roof above the quire and transept level. My eighteen years as a choirman at Saffron Walden had made me very familiar with John Wastell's stone mouldings!*

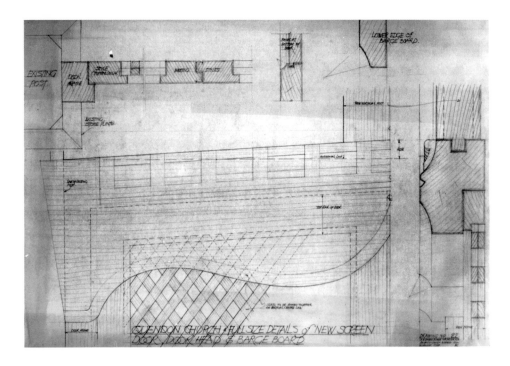

All this work was closely watched by Dykes Bower whenever he was not at the Abbey or elsewhere, and was usually to his approval, for I soon learned what was required. I 'filled him in' on discussions I had with the structural engineers and builder whenever he had not been present. One piece of advice I remember offering him, which was that the girth of the tower piers shown on Kirby's plan should be considerably increased, and in scale, SEDB readily agreed to.

In pure design matters, such as the arms of Archbishop Langton and the Magna Carta Barons to be applied to the stone shields round the walls of the quire above the arcades, and painted decoration in the ceilings above the quire, the transepts and under the organ, he would indicate what he had in mind and then leave me to produce the designs: for the transept ceilings, to take an example, he simply suggested birds for one and flowers for the other; the colour schemes he decided for himself, when the designs were done. In the same way I prepared, for his approval, designs for the carved oak choir stalls and the projecting organ loft; the pendant light fittings, and the embroidery of the high altar kneelers ... he invariably designed altar ornaments himself, to a small scale, sometimes for enlargement by me, and sometimes further refined here and there by him.[7]

above: Full size details of new screen door doorhead and bargeboard, drawn by Reginald Kirby, 1964

Mathew's frustration with Dykes Bower's working methods was tempered by admiration:

> It is certainly true that Dykes Bower exercised overall artistic control, but this did not seem burdensome because I, for one, very much admired his excellent taste and ability to create beautiful things with vitality as well as elegant refinement of shape, so there was no conflict between us, in design matters, that I can remember. I did notice that he often consulted F. C. Eden's fascinating sketchbooks, full of delicate architectural details he had gathered over the years.[8]

Notes

1   Letter from W. I. Croome to F. C. Eeles, 2 December 1950, Eeles papers, Church of England Record Centre.

2   Stephen Oliver, 'Stephen Dykes Bower, Architect: his Work at Magdalene College, Cambridge', *Magdalene College Magazine and Record*, no. 41, 1996–7, pp.34–43.

3   Letter from Hugh Mathew to Anthony Symondson, 2 March 1996.

4   Letter from Alan Rome to Anthony Symondson, 13 November 1995.

5   ibid.

6   Letter from Hugh Mathew to Anthony Symondson, 17 November 1995.

7   Letter from Hugh Mathew to Anthony Symondson, 15 February 1998.

8   Letter from Hugh Matthew to Anthony Symondson, 30 February 1998.

above: **The door screen at Quendon Church as executed**

Conclusion

At Quendon Court, Dykes Bower rose early and wrote letters, listened to the wireless solely for the weather, foreswore television and took *The Times*, reading mainly about architectural and Church affairs. He acquired an old Rolls Royce, painted maroon, which he drove like a tank through the lanes of Essex and used for site visits when not travelling by train. He spent part of each evening playing the piano; it kept his fingers supple. He enjoyed musical composition, although apart from Anglican chants little was performed publicly.

Visitors were met at Newport station and driven to Quendon in the car. Before lunch they were offered gin and French and sometimes, in the afternoon, taken to see local churches, returning for tea, after which they were conveyed to Newport for the train home. He continued to speak in sentences with the meticulous articulation of his youth, enjoyed good conversation, appreciated dry wit and dressed with understated elegance. His suits were made in Savile Row. Travel was one of his principal pleasures, and in old age he enjoyed reading travel books taken from the public library, lavishly illustrated in colour. He never lost his interest in architecture and gave valuable evidence in the St Pancras Hotel inquiry, but he did not believe that there would be another Gothic Revival. The word 'historicism' applied to traditional architecture was abhorrent to him. Another word he detested was 'reversibility'; to him this meant something that should not have been done in the first place. The candles in his candlesticks always tapered. He welcomed the foundation of the Kempe Society and accepted the presidency of the Ecclesiological Society. His ginger cat was called Mr Simpkin after the one belonging to the stoical craftsman from his home city, described by Beatrix Potter in *The Tailor of Gloucester*. He was terrified of bats. His garden was a solace, although he had little time for garden snobbery. In old age he would inspect it daily in a wheelchair, and not a weed was missed. Traditional buildings, he believed, were improved by well-chosen creepers. He was a member of the Oxford and Cambridge Club. He inspired awe and respect, but also deep affection in those who came to know him. He never married.

In his advancing years, a younger generation of architectural historians and critics came to see the value of the late Gothic Revival and twentieth-century traditional architecture as links in a chain of continuity. I met Dykes Bower in 1967 after receiving a letter inviting me to lunch at Little Cloister, Westminster Abbey, his London residence. It was occasioned by the restoration of St John's, Tue Brook, and a favourable article I had published in the *Architects' Journal* on the new Westminster Abbey lighting. This

opposite: Dykes Bower (centre) at Bury St Edmunds, 1992, with Peter Foster behind, Rodney Tatchell right

top: Decorated ceiling, Carlisle Cathedral quire
above: Underside of high altar canopy, St John's, Newbury

meeting led to a friendship of 27 years, founded on an appreciation of late-Victorian and Edwardian church architecture and its progression in the twentieth century.

While Dykes Bower felt isolated and suffered in silence the criticisms made of his work, his uniqueness and distinction were recognised by historians and critics such as David Watkin, Gavin Stamp, Alan Powers and James Stevens Curl. Paul Velluet wrote a student dissertation on his work. James Bentley, a clerical friend and writer who had used him to decorate Oldham parish church when he was vicar, also wrote about him.

In addition to his clerical patrons, two others in the Church of England encouraged his work. These were Michael Gillingham, an organ scholar and friend of John Dykes Bower, and Donald Findlay of the Central Council for the Care of Churches. Weekly, he talked on the telephone to Canon Wyatt. This predominantly conservative group admired his achievement and understood his objectives.

Many were surprised that Dykes Bower did not receive a knighthood in recognition of his work and distinction. Elizabeth Hoare, who ran Watts & Co., frequently lobbied Downing Street in his cause and obtained influential testimonials from his supporters. One was Sir John Betjeman who, on 26 January 1973, wrote to Edward Heath, the Prime Minister:

> *Stephen Dykes Bower is going to give up his work as Surveyor of the Fabric of Westminster Abbey in April when he reaches the age of seventy. He cleaned*

above: **Lancing College Chapel, the painted ceiling of the pulpitum**

*the stone there and brought colour and light into the building. At Bury St
Edmunds he built what I consider to be our finest modern Cathedral, for
he added to the east end of what was a parish church, choir and transepts
so harmoniously and subtly, that Bury Cathedral is a glory even of East
Anglia. His restoration work and original churchwork is well known. I would
particularly cite the beautiful organ case for Norwich Cathedral and the
restoration and new work which he did there. He is modest, self-effacing,
shy and when need be, deeply and dryly humorous. He is one of the great
men of architecture alive today, and I think that others would agree with
me, that he deserves recognition. I feel sure that the Dean and Chapter of
Westminster would support me, and all architects who are versed in the
tradition of English architecture as opposed to copiers of continental styles
and various forms of with-itry.*[1]

Despite support from Eric Abbott, Dean of Westminster, these efforts appeared to be
unavailing. According to J. M. Richards, Dykes Bower was offered a CBE but declined
it, explaining on one occasion that for purely personal reasons he did not want to be
honoured at a level lower than his brother, Sir John, believing that their achievements
were equal in their different spheres.

On Dykes Bower's ninetieth birthday in 1993, Donald Findlay secured for him a
Lambeth Doctorate of Literature, awarded by Archbishop Carey 'in recognition of
his outstanding contribution to church architecture for sixty years'. This pleased him
greatly. Part of Findlay's citation read:

*For him, architecture should speak of eternity, not of the present which
so soon becomes the past. What matters is that the design, whether the
baldacchino of St Paul's Cathedral, the whole of the eastern limb of Bury St
Edmund's Cathedral, a modest lych-gate in a Gloucestershire churchyard or
a pair of candlesticks in a Wren City church, should fall into place amongst
its surroundings.*[2]

Dykes Bower's ninetieth birthday was kept with Matins in Quendon church where
the Bishop of Chelmsford gave an appreciative address, and Dr John Birch of the Temple
Church in London and Dr Francis Jackson of York Minster played the organ. This was
followed by luncheon in the village hall attended by many friends, with speeches of
tribute to which he responded.[3]

He lived for another year, and died on 11 November 1994. The funeral took place in
Quendon church; Julian Litten provided a fine pall of black silk, designed by Comper
and embroidered with a figure of the Majestas, borrowed from St Cuthbert's, Philbeach
Gardens, Earls Court. The pall lay overnight on Dykes Bower's coffin, flanked by six
catafalque candlesticks. His body was cremated at Harlow at a service attended by
Warwick Pethers, Canon Wyatt and the author, and his ashes were buried in the floor of
the lower Islip Chapel in Westminster Abbey with those of others who had served the
abbey. Canon Wyatt preached at evensong when the ashes were interred.

Many saw Dykes Bower's death as the conclusion of a distinct episode in the history of the Church of England marked by education, learning and taste, in which the Book of Common Prayer, the King James Bible, and the Anglican choral tradition were all dignified, mysterious, resonant, powerful and historically sanctified symbols of a transcendent reality. Dykes Bower was an Anglican gentleman and devout High Church Tory with a love of England and an allegiance to Church and State. He was the closest living link with the Gothic style in English church architecture; he stood as the natural successor to the flower of Edwardian church architects. His fastidiousness and relentless quest for flawless perfection in architecture, combined with a quiet reticence, made him hard to please, but these were characteristics shared by his mentors. He was a private man with a horror of the limelight, and he asked only to be allowed to offer perfection through architecture and music in the worship of the Church of England. His dislike of the changes in the national Church did not deter him from contributing to what he regarded as its best interpretation. He was convinced that beauty would triumph as an indispensable characteristic of good architecture.

The ruthless scrapping of tradition under the sway of Modernism made any form of associationism in architecture and design nefarious, so that work in the historical styles was seen to be immoral for appearing to ignore the social and scientific demands of the modern age – hence the dismissal of Dykes Bower's work as 'architecture in fancy dress' and 'aping a past style'. Others, too, like Emmanuel Vincent Harris, Marshall Sisson, Raymond Erith, J. Sebastian Comper, Francis Johnson, McMorran & Whitby, Seely & Paget, Cecil Brown and W. Godfrey Allen were similarly tarred.

The effects on Dykes Bower were identified by Canon Wyatt in the latter's sermon in Westminster Abbey at his memorial service:

> Of set purpose this evening I have said very little about the pain of rejection which Stephen knew all through his working life. In the life of the Abbey here he found much happiness and large fulfilment in his work, but outside this place only too often his vision was repudiated and his work sabotaged and destroyed. Undoubtedly he felt pain: on one occasion after a particularly vicious attack he felt he might die; but even then his faith in God was such that it carried him through all temptation to despair.
>
> Stephen Dykes Bower has lived and practised his art in the most contra-dictory of times. There was a period of years when it seemed that he was the last of a great line of Gothic architects and the Church seemed to have turned its back on what is beautiful. We can be glad that Stephen lived even beyond his ninetieth year and received a Lambeth Doctorate from the Archbishop of Canterbury and warm tributes from many admirers. His struggle had not been in vain nor had it ended in defeat. His life and work, which spanned almost the whole of the twentieth century, will in my view, undoubtedly be studied and emulated in the future. The Church can no more turn its back on what is lovely and loving, gracious and good, than it can deny the unity of the Godhead or abandon the search for what is true or ignore the demand for what is holy.[4]

Nonetheless, Dykes Bower lived to see a change in the absolute ascendancy of Modernism. In 1972, J. M. Richards, his contemporary and former friend and an influential proponent of Modernism, was invited to give the annual discourse at the Royal Institute of British Architects and shocked many in the audience by questioning the policy of comprehensive development associated with the Modern Movement, as well as architects' eagerness for self-expression.[5] This was one of the first cracks to be seen in the Modernist edifice, and by the end of Dykes Bower's life a plural understanding of architecture, devoid of absolute values, brought greater sympathy towards his work so that it is now accepted as a valid part of the architectural achievement of his time.

Dykes Bower emphasised the imperative of beauty, and the value of continuity and style in place of originality and self-expression. He saw style in terms of language, with its own syntax and grammar and not pastiche or weak copyism, believing in the enduring value of the Classical and Gothic languages of architecture. A building by Dykes Bower is immediately unmistakeable despite his conscious avoidance of individualism. For all that he gathered the influences of J. N. Comper, Temple Moore and F. C. Eden and kept them alive through his work, nobody could mistake the quire and crossing of St Edmundsbury Cathedral as being by any hand other than his.

Warwick Pethers's majestic crossing tower stands as a vindication of the Dykes Bower tradition and the use of the Gothic style of architecture in the twenty-first

above: Weathercock for St Peter ad Vincula, Coggeshall

century. It is not only one of the finest buildings of the late twentieth century but the best and most permanent of the works brought into being by the Millennium Commission. It is a justification of Dykes Bower's work and principles unparalleled by no other. Moreover, his achievement in St Paul's and Westminster Abbey, now matured into sumptuous, unified splendour and order, provides a setting for state occasions and ceremonies known, by way of modern communications, throughout the world, as well as serving these great English churches with distinction and success.

Notes

1   Letter from Sir John Betjeman to Edward Heath, 26 January 1973, reprinted in Candida Lycett Green, ed., *John Betjeman: Letters, Volume Two: 1954 to 1984*, London, Methuen, 1995, p.458.

2   Anthony Symondson, ed., *S. E. Dykes Bower: A Birthday Celebration*, Quendon, 1994, p.1. This privately printed work contains the addresses given at Stephen Dykes Bower's birthday luncheon on 22 May 1993.

3   ibid.

4   'Sermon preached by the Reverend Canon D. S. C. Wyatt at the memorial service of STEPHEN ERNEST DYKES BOWER in Westminster Abbey on Monday 12 June 1995.' I am grateful to Warwick Pethers for lending me a copy of Canon Wyatt's sermon.

5   J. M. Richards, 'The Hollow Victory: 1932-72', Annual Discourse RIBA, *RIBA Journal*, May 1972, pp.132–76.

List of Works

This list was compiled by Robert Gladden from records in the Dykes Bower archive. Many unexecuted commissions and minor works have been omitted owing to lack of space. The date in the main heading is the date of Dykes Bower's appointment.

Note: for parish churches, the client is the incumbent and Parochial Church Council unless otherwise stated. For cathedrals, it is the Dean and Chapter. It has not been possible to obtain up-to-date information on the condition of most of the works listed. Mentions of works in *The Buildings of England* volumes are not included.

Substantially altered or partly demolished = *

Demolished = **

Unbuilt projects = ***

1931
Cottage
Lower Beeding, East Sussex
Client: Col. Sherringham

1931
St John the Baptist
Cirencester, Gloucestershire
Furnishing of Lady Chapel (Comper reredos expanded *c.*1948), restoration of rood screen and pulpit, Coronation and Second World War memorial tablets, alterations to layout of churchyard to west of the church and war memorial inscription in porch, completed 1953

1931–50
St Nicholas
Standish, Gloucestershire
New high altar, executed 1935; memorial in churchyard to Dykes Bower's parents, 1936; lychgate, west gallery and organ
Builder, 27 March 1931, p.563; 24 November 1933, p.818

1931–3
The College
Durham, Co. Durham
Alteration and decoration to organist's house
Client: John Dykes Bower

1931
***RIBA Building**
66 Portland Place, London
Competition entry with Robert Goodden

1931
***Curate's house**
Yorkley, Gloucestershire
Builder, 24 November 1932, pp.816 and 819

1932
St Bartholomew
Redmarley d'Abitot, Gloucestershire
Lady Chapel altar, tester and dorsal, ornaments
Builder, 24 November 1933, pp.818–9

above: Screen and font cover at west end, St Alban's, Copnor

1934–9
The Cathedral Church of Christ and St Mary
Durham, Co. Durham
Furnishing of Bede Altar in Chapel of the Nine Altars, altar hangings for high altar and Chapel of St Gregory
Builder, 7 June 1935, p.1052
The Times, 22 May 1935, p.10

1934–6
Quendon Court
Quendon, Essex
Client: Stephen Dykes Bower
Alterations and decoration of house; new garden office, 1957–8

1935–49
***St Mary**
Bedford, Bedfordshire
Restoration and reordering: installation of nave altar, resiting of organ in gallery at west end

top: Restored cottages at Ickleton
above: New cottages at Ickleton

1935
*****Cuddesdon College (now Ripon College, Cuddesdon)**
Cuddesdon, Oxfordshire
Competition for proposed new chapel; post-1945 scheme for enlargement of existing chapel
Architect and Building News, 7 June 1935, p.276

1935–75
The Cathedral Church of the Holy Trinity
Gloucester
Nave sanctuary hangings, ornaments; stairs and canopy for nave pulpit (no longer in place); recolouring of high altar reredos and the provision of new ornaments, hangings and sanctuary furniture; furnishing of Chapel of St Edmund as County War Memorial; furnishing of the Chapel of St John as memorial to Bishop Woodard; dorsal hanging for Lady Chapel, memorial tablets to Sir Fabian Ware (1950), Bishop Headlam (1947)
The Times, 11 June 1936, p.13; 12 June 1936, p.12

1935–7
All Saints
Hockerill, Hertfordshire
New church incorporating remains of fire-damaged 1851 structure; altar frontal, 1953
Architectural Association Journal, November 1937, pp.234–9
Builder, 14 January 1938, pp.85–8
Architectural Design and Construction, February 1938, pp.69 and 84
Fifty Modern Churches, London, Incorporated Church Building Society, 1947, pp.24–7

1935–8
Cottages
Ickleton, Cambridgeshire
Client: Capt. P. D. Mundy
In association with Hope Bagenal
Two terraces, of three and four workers cottages; restoration of the 'Town Housen'

1935–6
Alteration to house
22 Markham Street, London
Client: Mr J. E. H. Dykes

1936
St James
Wednesbury, Staffordshire
Major restoration, memorial tablet to Gertrude
Grigg

1936–8
St Nicholas
Hardwicke, Gloucestershire
Organ case, altar hangings

1936–7
St John
Shildon, County Durham
Refurnishing of chancel; removal of reredos
and provision of new altar with ornaments,
hangings and altar rails; screen to clergy vestry
in conjunction with resiting of side altar

1937–8
Holy Trinity
Bishops Stortford, Hertfordshire
Scheme of refurnishing, redecoration, reglazing
of chancel; new altar ornaments and hangings

1937–8
All Saints
Minstead, Hampshire
Lychgate

1937
Cottages
Quendon, Essex
Client: Sir W. Foot Mitchell
Pair of new semi-detached cottages and
conversion of existing pair into one

1937
Cottages
Ugley, Essex
Client: W. A. Tennant
Restoration and additions to existing cottages

1938–54
All Saints
Cottenham, Cambridgeshire
Decoration of chancel and new sanctuary
furnishings, English altar, candlesticks and altar
cross, altar rails; new lighting scheme, 1948–50

top: Lychgate, Minstead
above: Cottages at Quendon

1938
St Cyr
Stonehouse, Gloucestershire
Refurnishing of chancel; removing existing
reredos; lengthening altar to width of east
window with provision of new panelling, dorsal,
hangings and ornaments; removal of the stalls,
cancelli and altar rails and restoration of original
floor level and new altar rails

1938–2003
Quendon Parish Church
Quendon, Essex
Removal of dormers in nave roof and boarding of
nave ceiling; new wooden belfry, restoration of
porch, removal of Victorian windows from aisles
and substitution with new, reglazing of windows,
chancel panelling, decoration of chancel ceiling,
reredos, ornaments and hangings of high altar,
new lectern and stalls, new porch

1938–40
Cottages
Rickling Green, Essex
Client: H. Judd
Restoration of three agricultural workers'
cottages

1938–9
Cottage
Saffron Walden, Essex
Client: Saffron Walden Nursing Association

1938–9
House
Saffron Walden, Essex
Client: Dr and Miss C. Bartlett

1939–47
Cottages
Barnston, Essex
Client: Mr A. F. Graham Watson
Row of three agricultural workers' cottages

1939–43
All Saints
Cuddesdon, Oxfordshire
Client: The Principal of Cuddesdon College
Nave altar, sanctuary screens, altar hangings and
ornaments

1939–53
St Paul's Church
Willian, Letchworth, Hertfordshire
Extensive furnishing, including altar, ornaments
and hangings, rails, stalls, credence table and
font cover

1939–69
Cathedral Church of the Holy Trinity
Norwich
Consulting architect. Organ case, nave altar and
sanctuary; restoration of fabric of Bauchon, St
Andrew's and St Luke's chapels and Erpingham
Gate; refurnishing of Chapel of St Saviour (The
Royal Norfolk Regiment); restoration of the
Bishop's Throne; memorial tablets
The Times, 12 February 1940 (letter from
Andrew Freeman), p.4; 26
February 1940, p.6; 4 September 1942, p.6; 11
December 1953, p.5; 11 January 1960, p.14
Builder, 15 May 1940, pp.326 and 394

1939
Cottages
Wicken Bonhunt, Essex
Client: Mrs Bramwell Jackson
Pair of semi-detached tile-hung cottages

1940
St Peter ad Vincula
Great Coggeshall, Essex
Conservation of the war-damaged structure and
repair of the chancel for worship in 1940; resto-
ration of entire fabric: 1953–9
Norman Scarfe, *A Shell Guide, Essex*, London,
Faber & Faber, 1968, p.75Ya

1940
RAF Hullavington Chapel
Hullavington, Wiltshire
Design for the furnishing of chapel; altar,
hangings and ornaments

1943
St Laurence
Affpuddle, Dorset
Extensive refurnishing of the interior: triptych,
hangings and ornaments for high altar, new
organ case and west gallery, Lady Chapel altar
Executed 1947–50

1943–55
All Saints
North Cerney, Gloucestershire
Memorial to W. and E. Croome; new light
fittings, and repositioning of organ to west end

1943–90
St Edmundsbury Cathedral
Bury St Edmunds, Suffolk
See chapter 4
The Times, 23 August 1949, p.7; 5 April 1956,
p.4; 17 October 1956, p.12; 22 July 1957, p.5; 24
September 1970, p.5; 26 July 1997, p.11; 25 July
2005, p.49
Architects' Journal: Astragal column, 19 April
1956, pp.368–9; Alan Powers, 'Who owns archi-
tecture?', 12/19 December 1996, pp.26–7; Alan
Powers, 'Building Study: Bury St Edmunds', 8
September, pp.29–41
Builder, 15 June 1956, p.722
Architectural Review, June 1959, pp.431–2
Norman Scarfe, *The Suffolk Guide, Bury St
Edmunds*, Bury St Edmunds, The Alastair Press,
1988, p.64
Alan Powers, 'True Principles', *Crafts*, January–
February 1996, pp.22–5
Perspectives, February/March 1996, p.15
East Anglian Daily Times, 14 November 1997,
pp.1, 8, 26 and 28–9

'A Limestone Landmark', *Natural Stone*, August
2005, pp.16–22
Alan Powers, 'Triumph of Tenacity', *Spectator*, 8
October 2005, p.58
Gavin Stamp, 'Gothic revival', *Apollo*, May 2005,
pp.94–5

1944
St Mary the Virgin
Elham, Kent
Restoration of the church after war damage;
wooden south porch and parclose screen to the
north chapel, after sketch by F. C. Eden
Executed 1947–53

1944–60
**Cathedral Church of the Holy
Trinity**
Ely, Cambridgeshire
Consulting architect. Extensive restoration of
lantern and roofs, furnishing of new sanctuary
for the Lady Chapel, St Etheldreda's Chapel as
County War Memorial
The Times, 13 March 1952, p.6
RIBA Journal, September 1952, pp.397–401

1945–85
Cathedral Church of the Holy Trinity
Carlisle, Cumbria
Consulting architect. Border Regiment Chapel;
Chapel of St Wilfrid, including restoration of
Broughton Triptych; restoration of chancel roof
colouring; colouring of high altar baldacchino;
new ornaments, new quire desks and screens;
installation of pulpit from Cockayne Hatley,
Essex; new marble paving; new quire vestry
flanking nave. Unexecuted design for large
narthex at west end

Carlisle Cathedral altar ornaments, made by Frank Knight, 1966

1945–54

The Church of the Good Shepherd,
Par, Cornwall
Refurnishing of sanctuary, new high altar

1945

*Holy Spirit
Southsea, Hampshire
Major restoration of early twentieth-century church by J. T. Micklethwaite and Sir C. Nicholson after severe war damage. Furnished with stalls, font and pulpit salvaged from St Agnes', Kennington (G. G. Scott Junior, 1874–7; rood beam not installed); unexecuted fittings, e.g. organ case and Gothic baldacchino over high altar
Executed 1956–8
Substantially altered

1945–8

St John
Wotton, Surrey
Interior as war memorial; repaving, decoration of chancel roof, new altar, hangings and ornaments, triptych and altar rails, clergy stalls and desks; new door to vestry; relocation of organ to north chapel; war memorial plaque

1945–6

Cathedral Church of Christ and St Mary
Worcester
Advice on the proposed alterations and external treatment, design for the garden of No. 15 College Green; standard candlesticks for Lady Chapel, 1961

1945–62

St Mary the Virgin
Tilty, Essex
Pulpit, altar rails (now replaced), font, west window (by Pilgrim Wetton, 1952), tympanum with crucifix by Wetton, repair of west gallery for organ

1946

St Nectan
Ashcombe, Devon
Internal decoration and furnishing
Executed 1954–5

1946

St Nicholas
Castle Hedingham, Essex
Cross on east gable, 1951; repairs to fabric, memorial tablets
Executed 1966–85

1946–8

St Mary the Virgin
Eccles, Norfolk
Refurnishing of sanctuary

1946
St Nicholas
Great Yarmouth, Norfolk
Restoration and furnishing after war damage.
Executed 1953–69
The Times, 18 January 1953, p.3; 8 May 1961,
p.14; 25 August 1969, p.8; 2 July 1970, p.8
Whilhelmina Harrod, *A Shell Guide, Norfolk*,
London, Faber & Faber, 1982, p.186

1946–8
All Saints, Margaret Street
Westminster, London
Memorial brass to Dom Bernard Clements, OSB;
aumbry doors in bronze and silver

1946–52
King's College
The Strand, London
Chapel restored after war damage, tablet to
Bishop Headlam

1946
King's College Hostel
Vincent Square, London
Restoration of chapel after war damage
Executed 1950–2

1946–8
Holy Trinity
Meldreth, Cambridgeshire
Lighting scheme, restoration of tower and
chancel stonework
Executed 1956–62

1946–8
St Andrew
Quindenham, Norfolk
Refurnishing of lengthened sanctuary

1946–8
**St Stephen
Westminster, London
Refurnishing of east end after war damage; new
high altar, hangings and ornaments

1946–87
St James (Old Church)
Stanstead Abbots, Hertfordshire
Restoration after war damage, memorial tablets

1946–9
Cathedral Church of the Holy Trinity
Winchester, Hampshire
King's Royal Rifle Corps Memorial: alterations
and additions, and desk for Roll of Honour
Builder, 11 November 1949, p.602

1946
Winchester College
Winchester, Hampshire
New organ case
Executed 1951

1947–71
Christ Church Cathedral
Canterbury, Kent
Refurnishing of St John the Baptist Chapel and
Temple Memorial; restoration of marble altar,
flooring and ornaments; altar rails
The Times, 10 December 1948, p.7

1947–55
Cathedral Church of St. Peter
Exeter, Devon
Consulting architect. Restoration of the Bishop's
Throne and design for hanging; restoration and
conversion of the Bishop's Palace into diocesan
offices, library and bishop's residence after
government use during the war; restoration of
Bishop Oldham's Passage, linking the palace to
the cathedral

Everard monument, Great Waltham

1947
St Stephen, Linden Road
Gloucester
Altar, hangings and ornaments, dorsal and tester, in church by W. Planck, 1895. Altar ornaments now at St Mary Magdalene, Sherborne, Gloucestershire

1947
St Mary and St Lawrence
Great Waltham, Essex
Furnishing of north chapel as Everard Memorial Chapel, repainting of Everard monument. Executed 1957–9

1947
St Mary
Saffron Walden, Essex

Extensive restoration of the exterior stonework and timber roofs, redecoration of the interior and completion of the rood screen (by Sir Charles Nicholson)
Executed 1951–65

1948–55
St Paul's Cathedral
City of London
Competition design for new high altar and baldacchino, executed in association with the Cathedral Surveyor, W. Godfrey Allen. See chapter 2
Architect and Building News, 11 June 1848, pp.514–15; 7 May 1958, p.591
The Times, 1 June 1948, p.10; 29 November 1949, p.4; 1 March 1950, p.3; 9 May 1953, p.8; 16 October 1958, p.14; 18 November 1958, p.12
Architects' Journal, 17 June 1948, p.561; 4 June 1948, pp.662–4; 1 December 1949, p.640
Builder, 6 May 1949, p.553; 2 December 1949, pp.523–6; 30 May 1958, p.993; 28 November 1958, p.901
Architecture Illustrated, June 1949
Country Life, 1958, p.1231
Wood, July 1958, pp.88–9

Saffron Walden church, 1951

1948
St Paul
Charlestown, Cornwall
Extensive scheme of reordering and decoration
of interior, with sanctuary and chancel becoming
Lady Chapel
Executed 1951

1948
St Peter
East Blatchington, East Sussex
Redecoration and refurnishing of chancel;
repaving; decoration of roof; new high altar,
hangings, ornaments and stalls; floor slab in
memory of Revd Laing
Executed 1950

1948–62
St Vedast
Foster Lane, City of London
Restoration of Wren church incorporating Wren
furnishings from redundant City churches, new
clergy house with a courtyard linking to church
hall, 1691
Country Life (Mark Girouard), 2 June 1960,
pp.1254–5
The Times, 1 November 1967, p.12 (obituary of
Canon C. B. Mortlock)
Elain Harwood, *England, A Guide to Post-War
Listed Building*, London, Batsford, 2003, p.606
Alan Powers, *The Twentieth Century House in
Britain*, London, Aurum Press, 2004, pp.123–5

1948–51
St Augustine with St Philip
Stepney, London
Reordering of sanctuary of St Philip with
furnishings from St Augustine, and other
alterations
Executed 1950–1

1948
St Nicholas, Plumstead
Greenwich, London
Major refurnishing after war damage, with
triptych, hangings, ornaments and communion
rails of high altar; baldacchino, altar, hangings,
ornaments of Lady Chapel; altar, hangings and
ornaments of All Souls chapel; clergy stalls in
chancel, pulpit and font; quire stalls at west end
The structural restoration was undertaken by T.
F. Ford & Partners
Executed 1951–9

1948
St Chad
Middlesbrough, North Yorkshire
New church
Executed 1955–60

1948
St Peter and St Paul
Mitcham, Surrey
Restoration and partial redecoration of church
after war damage, with additional wall tablets
Executed 1950–1

1948
St Margaret
St Margaret-at-Cliffe, Kent
Restoration of tower and south aisle after war
damage, war memorial tablet
Executed 1952–4

1948
St Peter and St Paul
Shepton Mallet, Somerset
Refurnishing chancel, restoration of nave roof,
removal of organ from north chapel, furnishing
of Lady Chapel
Executed 1952–69

1948–56
St Mary
Stansted, Mountfitchet, Essex
Reglazing, removal of organ to west end,
furnishing of Lancaster chapel, memorial tablet
and memorial gates

1949–54
Pyes Fruit Farm
Barnston, Essex
Client: A. F. Graham Watson
New farm buildings and farm manager's house

1949–76
Cathedral Church of St Peter and St Cedd
Chelmsford, Essex
Consulting Architect. Interior decoration (roof
1961); reglazing; furniture and hangings, mostly
destroyed by reordering 1983–4. American
Memorial in south porch with stained glass by
Edward Woore
Stratford Express, 7 February 1958

1949–52
St Michael
Eastington, Gloucestershire
Refurnishing of chancel; new altar and triptych
altarpiece, hangings and ornaments, altar rail;
decoration of roof and furnishing of Lady Chapel
altar

1949–52
House
Great Chesterford, Essex
Client: Hon. Miss C. Neville

1949
St Nicholas
Guildford, Surrey
Redecoration of chancel and sanctuary of church
by Ewan Christian, restoration of reredos and
design of frontal and two sets of altar ornaments
Executed 1954–8

1949–52
St Mary
Hambleden, Oxfordshire
Refurnishing and redecoration of chancel
in memory of the 3rd Viscount Hambledon,
including altar ornaments in memory of Revd A.
H. Stanton

1949
Grosvenor Gardens
Westminster, London
Rifle Brigade Memorial

1949–63
St Martin-in-the-Fields
Westminster, London
Restoration of church after war damage;
furnishing of chapel in crypt in memory Revd
Dick Sheppard, with entrance arch and grille
as memorial to the 'Old Contemptibles' and
sanctuary lamp in memory of George Herriot

1949
St Mary the Virgin
Monken Hadley, Hertfordshire
Design for alteration of chancel as war memorial;
whitening of chancel walls and colouring of
ceiling, new hangings and altar cross; decoration
of panelling behind altar with ivory inlay

1949–66
St George, Wash Common
Newbury, Berkshire
Furnishing of church by F. C. Eden, including
baldacchino for the high altar based on design by
Eden, and for the Requiem and Lady chapels

1949
St George, Jesmond
Newcastle-upon-Tyne
Furnishing of War Memorial Chapel

1949
St Nicholas
North Walsham, Norfolk
Restoration of south porch and new oak doors
into the remains of the west tower
Executed 1953–5

1949–74
St Peter
Nottingham
Extensive refurnishing, with reordering of
sanctuary, removal of reredos, lengthening of
altar, new ornaments and hangings, and repositioning of organ; restoration of painted ceiling;
new pulpit; Spalding Memorial tablet

1949
St Mary and St Nicholas
Spalding, Lincolnshire
Rearrangement and redecoration of chancel,
boarding and decoration of the ceiling, alteration
of floor levels, lengthening of the high altar and
provision of new hangings, reglazing of side
windows in grisaille glass
Executed 1952–60

1949–53
Youngbury, High Cross
Ware, Hertfordshire
Agricultural workers' cottages and manager's
house
Executed 1951–3

1949–52
Cathedral Church of St Andrew
Wells, Somerset
Surveyor, 1949–55. Reports on Bishop's Palace;
lighting, restoration of stonework, high altar
rails, refurnishing of Chapel of St Martin, the
Somerset County War Memorial

1950–68
Magdalene College
Cambridge
Restoration, alteration and redecoration of
interior of chapel, including remodelling of organ
case and new desks with lights; major restoration of the exterior of first and second courts
and Pepys Building, river- and Bridge Street
elevations, with restoration of interior of Pepys
Building

1950–60
St Thomas
Craghead, Tyne and Wear
Redecoration of interior, partially executed
Henry Thorold, *A Shell Guide, Northumberland*,
London, Faber & Faber, 1980, p.76

1950–5
Rose Castle
Dalston, Cumberland
Client: Diocese of Carlisle
Alteration of the castle and grounds to make it
more practical, supervised on site by local archi-
tects Martindale & Jackson

1950
St Peter
Henfield, Sussex
Designs for refurnishing chancel, with new altar,
hangings and ornaments; alteration of the levels
and repaving of the floor; new altar rails

1950
Hurstpierpoint School
Hurstpierpoint, West Sussex
Client: The Woodard Foundation
Organ case
Executed 1962–4

1950–86
Lancing College
Lancing, West Sussex
Client: The Woodard Foundation
Completion of chapel, restoration of stonework
and reglazing of existing structure; antechapel
not executed
The Times, 10 June 1952, p.7; 14 October 1976,
p.4; 6 January 1981, p.1
Builder, 13 June 1952, p.872; 16 June 1958, p.993
Country Life, 2 July 1953, pp.48–50
Stephen Dykes Bower, 'The Rose Window at
Lancing', *Journal of the British Society of Master
Glass-Painters*, 1978–9, pp.31–6
Basil Handford, *The History of Lancing Chapel*,
pamphlet, *c*.1978, printed with illustrations
in *Architecture*, Journal of the Society for
Architecture, Autumn 1975, pp.36–41

1950–3
St Michael, Cornhill
City of London
Repairs after war damage to Wren church

1950
St John
Newbury, Berkshire
New church on the site of bombed church by
William Butterfield; built 1954–7, furnishing
continued until 1963
Brick Bulletin, March 1959, p.3; December 1959,
p.9
Elain Harwood, *England, A Guide to Post-War
Listed Building*, London, Batsford, 2003, p.374

1950–1
St German, Roath
Cardiff
Statue of St German

1950
***Cathedral Church of SS Peter and Paul**
Sheffield
Schemes of enlargement, unexecuted

1950
St Cuthbert
Wells, Somerset
Restoration of the medieval roofs, with
decoration of the nave roof
Executed 1959–62; altar frontal, 1964
Wells Journal, 5 February 1960

1951–66
Holy Trinity
Barkingside, Essex
Pair of fald stools, vestries at the west end, font
and aumbry

1951–4
St Mary Arches
Exeter, Devon
Restoration and rearrangement of chancel after
war damage (in library use)

1951
St Michael
Farway, Devon
Furnishing of Lady Chapel with new stone altar,
dorsal, hangings and ornaments, credence table
and marble flooring

1951–9
Drinking Fountains
Central London
Designs in several locations for the Metropolitan
Drinking Fountain and Cattle Trough
Association: Old Palace Yard, 1954; Kew Gardens
(proposed standard design), 1955; Hyde Park,
1957; Trafalgar Square, 1959; new standard
design, 1959
The Times, 14 April 1959, p.11

1951–72
**Collegiate Church of St Peter
(Westminster Abbey)**
London
Work as described in chapter 3
Builder, 29 June 1951, p.911; 22 January 1965,
pp.207–10
The Times, 3 February 1953, p.3; 24 August 1953,
p.8; 27 October 1953, p.5; 18 November 1953,
p.3; 4 December 1953, p.4; 15 January 1954, p.5;
9 April 1954, p.10; 25 June 1954, p.2; 31 August
1954, p.3; 23 December 1955, p.10; 14 February
1956, p.5; 25 October 1956, p.12; 18 February
1957, p.5; 23 October 1957, p.11; 9 March 1960,
p.14; 2 February 1963, p.10; 3 March 1965, p.5;
18 May 1966, p.12; 11 February 1967, p.9; 18
February 1967, p.13; 28 February 1967, p.11

1952–66
Queens' College
Cambridge
Restoration of painted decoration of chapel
and alterations to altar; restoration of painted
decoration of hall; proposed new range between
River Cam and Fruit Tree Court (1955),
unexecuted
John Twigg, *A History of Queens' College,
Cambridge, 1448-1986*, Woodbridge, Boydell
Press, 1987, p.373

1952–5
St Martin
Canterbury, Kent
Redecoration of chancel, with new dorsal for high
altar; nave relit
The Times, 22 January 1954, p.8

1952–67
St Andrew
Quatt, Shropshire
Extensive structural repair, including under-
pinning chancel and rebuilding and interior
restoration of Walryche Chapel; reordering of

interior; redecoration, reglazing and repaving;
cleaning and colouring of tombs; memorial
tablets; removal of organ to new west gallery;
new pews in nave

1953–64
St Andrew
Ashburton, Devon
Font cover, not in the original scheme; high altar
ornaments; wrought-iron and glass gates in north
porch, with memorial tablet

1953–5
St Mary's
Baldock, Hertfordshire
Refurnishing of sanctuary and high altar: new
hangings and ornaments

1953–68
Church of The Good Shepherd
Arbury, Cambridgeshire
New church (originally intended to be dedicated
to St Nicholas Ferrar), rectory and church
hall, built and furnished in two stages: chancel
followed by nave
The west end was completed by Cecil J. Bourne,
1975
Norman Scarfe, *A Shell Guide, Cambridgeshire*,
London, Faber & Faber, 1983, p.108

1953–64
St Peter
Limpsfield, Surrey
Redecoration and refurnishing of interior,
including whitening of interior, repaving
and refurnishing of sanctuary, boarding and
decoration of chancel ceiling, new organ and
other furnishing

1953

Chelsea Physic Garden

Kensington and Chelsea, London

Restoration of statue of Sir Hans Sloane

1953–6

St Mark, Marylebone

Westminster, London

Refurnishing of sanctuary with new high altar, hangings and ornaments; former high altar moved to south chapel

1953–6

Emilie Agnes Elin Almshouses

Meldreth, Cambridge

Client: Miss M. Bowen

1953–6

Holy Trinity

Nuware Eliya, Ceylon

Altar ornaments

1953–7

Magdalen College

Oxford

Restoration of exterior stonework of Founder's Tower and St Swithun Building

The Times, 25 May 1954, p.10

1954–6

St Ia

St Ives, Cornwall

Baptistery

1954–5

The Cathedral of the Holy and Undivided Trinity

Peterborough, Cambridgeshire

Standard candlesticks for high altar in memory of Bishop Blagdon

1954–70

St Paul

Spennymoor, Co. Durham

Restoration of 1858 Victorian church after fire, with new vestry and copper pyramid cap to the tower, new furnishing, stained glass, advice on organ case

Henry Thorold, *County Durham, a Shell Guide*, London, Faber & Faber, 1980, p.166

1954–83

Guild Chapel

Stratford-upon-Avon, Warwickshire

Extensive restoration, refurnishing and redecoration

1954–67

St James

Thorley, Hertfordshire

Restoration of the roofs, timber spire, pews and timber flooring; external and internal whitewashing

1955–7

St John the Baptist

Royston, Hertfordshire

New presbytery

1956

St Andrew

Currey Rivel, Somerset

Refurnishing of chancel; quire stalls, communion rails and organ case

1956

St Mary

Little Chart, Kent

Ornaments for high altar; processional cross, 1963

1956

Dudmaston Hall

Quatt, Shropshire

Advisor in the restoration

Executed 1962–6

1957–8

St Mary

Barnsley, Gloucestershire

Memorial tablet to Mrs L. Verey

1957–8

Conversion of cottages to single house

Lofts Hall, Wendon Lofts, Essex

Client: Mr A. F. Graham Watson

Clad in timber shingles

1957–8

***St Columba

Middlesbrough, North Yorkshire

Unexecuted schemes for new rectory and church
hall

1957–8

Merton College

Oxford

Repairs to Mob Quad, and enlargement and
alteration of library

1957–8

University College

Oxford

Reconstruction and restoration of the south
range (hall and chapel elevations) of Front Quad

1957–78

St Mary

Sanderstead, Surrey

Reglazing of sanctuary and Lady Chapel
windows; lectern, 1962; completion of west end
with first-floor parish rooms, 1970–1; other
works, to 1978

1957–67

St John

Weston-super-Mare, Somerset

Reordering and redecoration of chancel,
removing wrought-iron screen and moving organ
to west gallery, repaving chancel, new altar rails
and stalls

1958

St Mary

Fairford, Gloucestershire

Stone paving in nave

1958–62

Holy Trinity

Darlington, Co. Durham

Redecoration and refurnishing of chancel and
south aisle altar in church by Anthony Salvin,
1838, with new high altar and dorsal; bronze and
wrought-iron altar rails

1958–60

Holy Trinity

Fareham, Hampshire

Scheme of redecoration for interior of church by
J. Owen, 1834–7; interior repaved and reglazed,
font moved and the sanctuary refurnished

1958–61

Rugby School Chapel

Rugby, Warwickshire

Cleaning, redecoration and refurnishing
of chapel by William Butterfield, 1870–2;
decoration of roof, alterations to altar and
reredos – new ornaments, new organ case and
console and grilles to organ loft, small works in
antechapel, resiting memorial tablets

1958–62
Christ Church
Sutton, Surrey
Pews, desks and altar rails for Lady Chapel

1958
St Andrew and St Mary
Watton-at-Stone, Hertfordshire
Rearrangement of east end, decoration of interior
and repositioning of organ

1958
***The Minster
Wimborne Minster, Dorset
Design for organ case
Unexecuted

1959–83
Felstead School Chapel
Felstead, Essex
Enlargement of chapel by F. Chancellor, 1873
with transepts by A. E. Munby, 1926, with new
east and west ends and additional transepts
and fleche over crossing. Interior redesigned
with colouring of organ case and glazing of apse
windows with fragmentation glass, west screen
with stalls incorporating war-memorial painting
by F. O. Salisbury, 1921

1959–81
Christ Church Cathedral
Oxford
Refurnishing of interior with reglazing of the
clerestory and lantern; repaving; cleaning interior
stonework; restoration of memorial tablets;
relighting, with new pendant lighting; high altar
reredos restored with new hangings and standard
candlesticks; Latin Chapel restored, refurnished and decorated; refurnishing of altar of St
George's Chapel; memorials to Archbishop Paget
and General Paget

Christ Church Cathedral, Oxford, after cleaning in
1962

1959–67
Proposed New Church
South Redcar, North Yorkshire
Proposed new church for South Redcar, a new
suburb of the town. The first design rejected in
1962; second, cheaper, design submitted 1965
and rejected in 1967

1959–60
Public Garden
Church Street, Saffron Walden, Essex

c.1960
St Peter
Birch, Essex
Quire stalls and seats (two of these now in St
Edmundsbury Cathedral)

1960–78
St Michael
Bishops Stortford, Hertfordshire
Restoration of fabric, cleaning and redecoration
of interior, refurnishing of high altar

1960–9
St Michael
Chagford, Devon
Redecoration and refurnishing, paving of chancel
and sanctuary and restoration of Victorian
triptych, construction of ringers' platform and
screen under tower to provide vestry on ground
floor, new organ case, decoration of parclose
screens and Lady Chapel roof, designs for
stained-glass windows

1960–3
All Saints
Flore, Northamptonshire
Redecoration and refurnishing with new lighting,
repair and replastering of chancel, whitewashing
of interior, sanctuary refurnished with new high
altar, hangings and ornaments, communion
benches, chancel roof decorated; new pulpit
stairs, 1985

1960–78
St Peter and St Paul
Hellingly, Sussex
Furnishing of Lady Chapel, high altar ornaments,
repairs to stonework

1960–5
St Mary
Selly Oak, West Midlands
Internal redecoration and refurnishing of 1860s
church by E. Holmes

1960
The College of the Ascension
Selly Oak, Birmingham
Design for high altar, including frontal, gradine
and tester

1960
St Mary
Tenby, Pembrokeshire
Colouring of roofs, construction of interior porch
and opening up of blocked medieval window

1961–3
St Oswald
Ashbourne, Derbyshire
Decoration of the chancel roof, quire desks lamps

1961–5
St Nicholas
Great Wakering, Essex
Restoration and partially realised reordering and
refurbishing of interior

1961–3
St John
Harpenden, Hertfordshire
Lady Chapel addition to east end of church
by F. C. Eden, 1908; furnishing and decora-
tions

1961–3
All Saints
Hawley, Surrey
Redecoration of interior, alteration to high altar,
restoration of reredos

1961
***The Royal College of Arms
City of London
Scheme for a museum adjacent to the college
Unexecuted

1961–6
Merchant Taylor's Hall
City of London
Design for organ case for east end of hall, utilising a Renatus Harris organ of 1724 originally from St Dionis, Blackchurch, London; advice on library

1961–79
St Alban
Copnor, Portsmouth, Hampshire
Extensive scheme of decoration, furnishing and reordering of the interior of church by Sir Charles Nicholson, 1914

1961–5
New Rectory
Quendon, Essex
Client: The Church Commissioners

1961–2
Christchurch Cathedral
Victoria, British Columbia, Canada
Stone tablet to commemorate the gift in 1929 of a Sir George Gilbert Scott iron screen from Westminster Abbey

1961–9
St Mary
Woodbridge, Suffolk
Repair of the church; design of new light fittings, lectern and a proposed reconstruction of the organ

1962–6
St John's College
Cambridge
Decoration and lighting of college dining hall and staircase to senior common room

1962–7
St Laurence
Hawkhurst, Kent
Font cover, ornaments for high altar

1962–5
St Mary
Horsham, Sussex
Redecoration, relighting and reglazing; refurnishing of Holy Trinity Chapel; decorated ceiling, new altar hangings, ornaments and gradine, seating

1962–79
St Mary the Virgin
Newport, Essex
Interior repaved and whitewashed, wrought-iron altar rails

1962–5
Trinity College
Oxford
New organ case for chapel

1962–8
St Michael
Bishopwearmouth, Co. Durham
Redecoration of interior and refurnishing of sanctuary with new high altar hangings and ornaments

1962–4
Eton College
Eton, Berkshire
Rifle Brigade War Memorial in cloisters

1963
Holy Cross
Daventry, Northamptonshire
Major restoration of church by David Hiorns,
1752–8; designs for furnishings include: lighting
hoops; lectern; and the furnishing of a side
chapel with altar table, ornaments, hangings and
kneelers

1964–9
St Peter and St Paul
Hambledon, Hampshire
Redecoration and refurnishing of chancel, new
lighting

1964–5
The Chapel
Knole House, Sevenoaks, Kent
Redecoration of chapel including ceiling, altar
frontal

1965–7
St Mary the Virgin
Prittlewell, Essex
Decoration of chancel roof, new altar ornaments
for the Jesus Chapel

1966–8
Corpus Christi College
Cambridge
New organ case for chapel

1966–71
St John, Tue Brook
Liverpool
Restoration of painted interior of church by G.
F. Bodley, 1867–70; Chapel of the Holy Cross
formed under west tower, using Bodley's screen
from Dunstable Priory, 1977–80
Architects' Journal, 25 June 1975, pp.1300–1

1966–70
St Lawrence
Rowehedge, Essex
Scheme for reordering of polygonal nineteenth-
century church with the installation of Classical
altarpiece from Minster, Sheppey, and font from
St Martin's, Colchester, Essex

1966–73
St Mary
Turweston, Berkshire
Repair of stonework, limewashing of interior and
reglazing, new lectern.

1966–73
St Augustine
Westbury, Berkshire
Reglazing and redecoration, alteration to
sanctuary, lowering of footpace and removal of
reredos

1967–70
St Elvan
Aberdare, Mid Glamorgan
Reordering, with nave sanctuary, altar hangings
and ornaments; chancel becoming the Lady
Chapel; decoration of the chancel roof;
furnishings

1967–77
St Stephen, Prenton
Birkenhead, Cheshire
Furnishing and decoration of Lady Chapel

1967–8
St Peter
Duntisbourne Abbots, Gloucestershire
Clergy stall and Bishop's Chair, with accompa-
nying desks. Possibly unexecuted

1967–86
St Mary the Virgin
Gamlingay, Bedfordshire
Major restoration of the fabric, including
reglazing of the church

1967–78
St Paul, Paddington
Salford, Manchester
Major restoration and reordering of church by E.
H. Shellard, 1856, with new parish hall, rectory
and enclosed garden; furnishing continued until
1986
Country Life, 17 April 1986, pp.1026–7

1967–9
All Saints
Newmarket, Suffolk
Pendant lights

1967–8
St Peter, Southsea
Portsmouth, Hampshire
Furnishing of Lady Chapel, candelabra in chancel

1967–78
St Andrew
West Kirby, Cheshire
Redecoration of church by John Douglass,
1889–1909; restoration of the high altar reredos,
removal of the chancel screen and the installation and decoration of the font cover from St
Paul, Birkenhead, furnishing of Requiem Chapel
altar

1968–9
St George
Douglas, Isle of Man
Redecoration of sanctuary; removal of reredos;
new altar, hangings and ornaments

1968–76
St John the Baptist
Newcastle-upon-Tyne
Scheme for reordering, restoration and redecoration; reglazing and paving of nave; cleaning of
internal stonework; nave sanctuary; decoration
of the pulpit, font cover and former high altar
reredos; wrought-iron chancel screen

1968–71
St James
Tunbridge Wells, Kent
Redecoration and minor reordering of the
sanctuary by Ewan Christian, 1862; removal of
reredos, panelling of walls, new altar hangings
and cross

1968–70
St Clement
Great Ilford, Essex
Sanctuary furniture

1968–76
All Saints
Laleham, Middlesex
Refurnishing of chancel; new altar, hangings,
ornaments and altar rail; two-decker pulpit and
stalls

1970–6
St John
Stansted, Essex
Advice on decoration, installation of new glass,
cleaning and painting interior

1971
Holy Trinity
Hildersham, Cambridgeshire
Restoration of Victorian mural paintings in
chancel

1971–4
St Laurence
Wormley, Hertfordshire
Structural work; furnishings: new font cover,
altar ornaments and quire desks

1971–7
St Augustine
Pendlebury, Manchester
Repairs and restoration

1972
St Andrew
Penrith, Cumberland
Consultant on restoration; decorative scheme for
interior

1973–5
Holy Trinity
Dartford, Kent
Furnishing reinstated medieval chapel of St
Thomas à Becket

1973–6
St Mary with St Peter
Oldham, Lancashire
Reordering and redecoration of interior of 1820s
Georgian Gothick church by Richard Lane

1973–9
The Church of the Holy Cross
Woodchurch, Birkenhead, Cheshire
Redecoration of interior: refurnishing of nave
sanctuary with new ornaments, hangings and
altar rails; chancel became a chapel with new
altar and ornaments; decoration of screen
to organ chamber and war memorial, set of
vestments (1983) and paschal candlestick (1984)

1975–7
Holy Trinity
Pleshey Bridge, Essex
1945 reordering scheme partially realised, with
reglazing, redecoration and new lighting

1977–8
St Mark, Dundela
Belfast
Redecoration of William Butterfield church,
1878, with new lighting and desk lights for the
quire, and other minor items of furniture

1977–8
The Cathedral Church of the Holy Trinity
Chichester, West Sussex
Furnishings in the Bishop Kemp Chapel

1979–82
Holy Trinity
Drumbo, Lisburn, Co. Antrim
Redecoration and relighting

1980
St Margaret
Hinton Waldrest, Berkshire
Airey Neave Memorial Window, made from
Victorian fragments by John Lawson of Goddard
& Gibbs

1980–2
St John the Evangelist
Higher Broughton, Manchester
Desk lights for quire stalls.

1981
St Malachi
Hillsborough, Lisburn, Co. Antrim
Desk lights for quire stalls.

1981–8
Christ Church
Moss Side, Manchester
Restoration and installation of fittings from other churches; see chapter 6
The Times, 5 June 1981

1990–2
St Peter
Hale, Cheshire
Altar frontal

Dates unknown
(alphabetical order by location)
St Mary
Doddington, Cambridgeshire
New north porch

St Michael and All Angels
Eastington, Gloucestershire
High Altar
David Verey, *A Shell Guide, Gloucestershire,* London, Faber & Faber, 1970, p.76

Holy Trinity
Eltham, London
Extensive furnishing, memorial to Revd Hall, some alteration to structure

St Andrew
Hingham, Norfolk
Design for new high altar, hangings and ornaments, and rails

St Leonard
Leverington, Cambridgeshire
Designs for an organ case and refurnishing of south (Swaine) chapel

St Giles
Norwich
Interior furnishings

St Swithun
Sandford, Devon
Reordering and refurnishing lighting scheme

St Mary the Virgin
Tilty, Essex
Pulpit and altar rails

St John
Wakefield, West Yorkshire
Organ case in new west gallery chapel, formed in former organ chamber

St Mary
Whorlton, Co. Durham
Design for grave slab to Bishop Headlam in churchyard

Obituary

Stephen Dykes Bower, *The Times*, 1994

Stephen Dykes Bower was that rare figure among contemporary architects – although not so rare in the 19th century where many of his allegiances lay and where temperamentally he often seemed to belong – an architect whose interests and whose practice were wholly ecclesiastical. For 22 years from 1951 he held the post of Surveyor of the Fabric of Westminster Abbey, and he was a competent and knowledgeable designer in the Gothic style, having been responsible for several notable works including the enlargement of Bury St Edmunds Cathedral and the completion of Lancing College chapel.

Stephen Ernest Dykes Bower was the second son of Ernest Dykes Bower, a prominent doctor in the city of Gloucester. His was a musical family. Stephen's younger brother, who became Sir John Dykes Bower, achieved distinction as an organist and eventually held the post of organist of St Paul's Cathedral; and Stephen himself on leaving Cheltenham College went to Merton College, Oxford, as organ scholar. While at Oxford, however, he decided not to pursue a musical career but to take up architecture – the study of Gothic churches having already become for him an absorbing interest.

In 1924 he entered the Architectural Association School in London, where his designs had a Gothic bias from the beginning and led to his being somewhat out of step with the then current architectural fashions. He spent several vacations in the 1920s travelling with a fellow student studying the French Gothic cathedrals.

Dykes Bower took his diploma in 1931 and began his own architectural practice forthwith, concentrating on church building and restoration. He worked at several of the English cathedrals as well as on Oxford and Cambridge colleges. He was also architect for the cathedral library and bishop's palace at Exeter, for the restoration of Great Yarmouth parish church and (after its severe damage by bombing during the war) for the restoration of the Wren church of St Vedast, Foster Lane, in the City of London. He also collaborated with Godfrey Allan over the design of the new high altar in St Paul's Cathedral after the Victorian reredos had been destroyed by a high explosive bomb, and over the postwar baldacchino and American memorial chapel.

Dykes Bower showed himself happiest, however, with Gothic designs, and his two most notable works at Bury St Edmunds and Lancing, though thought by some to be lacking in vigour, demonstrated his knowledge and understanding of medieval ways of building.

It was this knowledge that enabled him to make a success of his surveyorship at Westminster Abbey, though his time in that post was not without its misjudgments.

His proposal, for example, to replace the old stone slabs forming the floor of the nave with a patterned tiled floor designed by himself caused much controversy and was eventually withdrawn, even though it had been approved by the Dean and Chapter.

He was simultaneously consulting architect to Carlisle Cathedral (1947-75) and in 1983 was elected President of the Ecclesiological Society.

Stephen Dykes Bower was a withdrawn and unaggressive character whose firm opinions were disguised by his scholarship and precise Victorian manner. He played little part in professional politics.

He never married and pursued a rather uneventful existence, enriched by his continuing devotion to music in the elegant house where he also had his office at Quendon in Essex, which he occupied for most of his life.

SIR JAMES RICHARDS
THE TIMES, 14 NOVEMBER 1994

Obituary

Stephen Dykes Bower, *Churchscape*, 1995

During his student days that wonderful, but much underrated architect F. C. Eden (1864–1944) had befriended the young Dykes Bower, dined him in Bedford Square, and even took him to Italy. Eden, Walter Tapper and W. I. Croome (later Chairman of the Cathedral's Advisory Committee) often spent architectural holidays on the Continent together; Eden's masters had been G. F. Bodley and Thomas Gardner, giving a direct line of succession to Dykes Bower from the greatest ecclesiastical architects of the late nineteenth century.

On leaving the AA he found that in the Depression there was little work about, so he went into a Chelsea office and then took a job in the Great Western Railway, drawing office; although he was extremely knowledgeable about locomotives and always loved trains, he greatly disliked the station architecture of P. E. Culverhouse upon which he was employed.

He went to see Sir Walter Tapper, at that time Surveyor of Westminster Abbey, but without success. Fortunately a relative gave him a commission in the country and he started his own practice. In 1933 Dr Ernest Dykes Bower died and Stephen and his formidable mother bought Quendon Court, a beautiful eighteenth-century house near Saffron Walden. In 1936 fire virtually destroyed All Saints, Hockerill, not far from Quendon: Dykes Bower was asked to prepare designs for the new church and his ecclesiastical career was launched. Not that this was at all unexpected: by the age of 11 he was able to draw all the English cathedrals from memory and his musical and compositional abilities were allied to a consuming interest in organs and organ cases at a time when, since the deaths of Bodley and Pearson, case design was hardly studied at all save by a few architects such as W. D. Caröe or Tapper.

In addition to being a gifted composer, pianist and organist, Dykes Bower had a superb command of the English language evident in the reviews and papers which he wrote for the *RIBA Journal* during the 1930s. One review of a paper by Comper on the English Altar, brought him to the attention of that notable liturgiologist and architect, and another entitled 'Organs and Organ Cases' should be read by any architect aspiring to design an organ case. In a critique in the *Architect and Building News* of Leslie Moore's new Lady Chapel, added to his father-in-law's wonderful conception St Wilfrid's, Harrogate, Dykes Bower imparts wise advice and reveals what was to be his lifelong view of architecture, firmly held despite all criticisms, hostility and professional ostracism:

'St Wilrid's, Harrogate, is a reminder of what is too often disregarded – that what we need today is not so much originality as quality. It is given to very few people to be really original, and it is much better that people should not try; in fact for the ordinary

man to try is usually to court disaster. The average architect need not aspire to be
a prophet: he will do very well if he succeeds in being an artist. There has been too
much attention paid to the *matter* and not enough to the *manner*. While no one would
under-estimate the importance of what an artist has to say – it is obviously essential
that it should be intelligent – how it is said is perhaps more important, since unless it
is reasonably competent, the artist is not an artist at all. If some of the labour devoted
to saying something new was devoted to saying something well, everything would
no doubt take a little longer and seem a good deal harder, but it would certainly be
a great deal better and more worth having. Fashions change with such rapidity that
a reputation for originality can at best be short lived. It is the quality of the work, its
inherent architectural value that alone gives life and permanent pleasure.'

When it was unfashionable to do so, Dykes Bower consistently stood up for
nineteenth-century architects and artists, such as Kempe and Clayton & Bell, and
composers – Sterndale Bennett, Stainer, Sullivan and Parry.

The outbreak of War temporarily put an end to normal architectural practice and
Dykes Bower served with the Ministry of Town and Country Planning in the regional
commission at Cambridge.

At the end of the War, he re-started his practice with the repair and replanning
of the Bishop's palace in Exeter and in 1948/9 he won the competition to replace the
reredos by Bodley and Garner at St Paul's Cathedral. The *RIBA Journal* for December
1948 published the Dykes Bower design with beautiful drawings by Reginald Kirby; with
typical generosity the then Surveyor, Godfrey Allen, was asked to be associated with the
project.

The great work was completed as the architect intended, though there were battles
over the chandeliers and the altar cross. The 1948 drawings showed an extremely large
high altar cross which would have been clearly visible from a great distance. A move
was made to reduce this to a two-foot high ornament; after a protracted battle the
present compromise, which tends to lose the cross against the Brian Thomas glass, was
reached. The very successful glass embodies all that Dykes Bower held to be important
– relatively small scale, good colour, firm design, and respect for the architecture.

Stephen Dykes Bower's energy was combined with prolific output. Although a
catalogue of works is generally to be avoided in a tribute of this sort, so much was
achieved that it is inevitable. Much of this work is so well matched to its setting that it is
often overlooked.

Westminster Abbey – restoration of tombs, Pearson organ cases, Blore pulpitum, choir
stalls, Scott reredos, fabric generally, vestments, ornaments etc;

St Paul's Cathedral – baldacchino (ciborium), high altar, American Memorial
Chapel;

Norwich Cathedral – furnishing of Norfolk Regiment Chapel, St Saviour's Chapel,
new organ case, restoration of medieval throne, restoration of medieval choir stalls and
Victorian choir stalls, etc;

Carlisle Cathedral – Border Regiment Chapel and general refurnishing;

St Nicholas Great Yarmouth – rebuilding of the largest parish church in England following virtual destruction during the war, including design of every fitting down to hinges and door handles, chalices, candlesticks and embroidery;

St Edmundsbury Cathedral – new choir and transepts specially designed to incorporate beautiful existing nineteenth century glass by Kempe, Clayton & Bell and Hardman (a thoroughly misunderstood design for this reason);

Lancing College Chapel – a completion of R. C. Carpenter's enormous chapel;

Chelmsford Cathedral – restoration and redecoration;

Peterborough Cathedral – superb silver gospel lights;

Wells Cathedral – altar rails (wrongly sited which led to resignation);

University College, Oxford – restoration of medieval buildings;

Christ Church Cathedral, Oxford – embellishment, new altar ornaments and lowering of Bodley's reredos;

Magdalene College, Cambridge – restoration of medieval buildings;

St Vedast, Foster Lane, London – rebuilding after bomb damage and new rectory (one of the best new buildings in the City);

Queens' College, Cambridge – restoration of Bodley decoration scheme in the chapel;

Canterbury Cathedral – William Temple Memorial Chapel;

Gloucester Cathedral – nave altar and ornaments, decoration of Scott reredos, tombs, pulpit, canopy, etc.;

Felsted School – designs for the completion of chapel;

Rugby School – organ case, grille and fittings in Butterfield chapel.

To this list could be added parish church fittings and restorations all over the country, and new churches such as St John's, Newbury.

In all these schemes Dykes Bower's ideas were ably interpreted and incomparably well drawn by the late Reginald Kirby and by John O'Neilly, Hugh Mathew and in latter years Warwick Pethers. Working for Stephen was enormously rewarding and I have treasured letters from him. 'Your drawings for Shefield were very well received ...' 'I have brought back the Lancing drawings so that you can proceed with completing the sections ... 'The drawings were an invaluable help in explaining the proposals.'

Prominent among the draughtsmen, artists and craftsmen were: Eric White and George Coburn of Longleys of Crawley, Mr Haslop of Rattee and Kett (joiners and carvers), W. J. Butchart (trained by Comper), Campbell Smith (Decorators and gilders), Frank Knight of Wellingborough, Messrs Howard Brown of Norwich (silversmiths), Brian Thomas, Powells of Whitefriars, Mr Buss and Mr Lawson of Goddard and Gibbs (stained glass), Watts & Co Ltd., Mrs Ozanne (fabrics and needlework), Wainwright & Waring; and Mr Furneaux (metalworkers), and there were of course many others.

In his exceptionally perceptive obituary, Fr Anthony Symondson referred to the unfair treatment meted out to him in the Westminster Abbey roof controversy. 'He became the victim of two forces, the ideology of the Modern Movement and the narrowing restrictions of conservation. Both were inimical to the educated and literate

standards of architecture of which he was a Master'. (His opinions on certain doctri-
naire conservationists and official bodies are unrepeatable here.)

His views were trenchantly summed up in a letter written to me in January 1970:

'frank restoration – the total absence of any recognizable architectural language is
all that some architects are capable of today … one of the reasons indeed why I view this
fashionable word "conservation" with suspicion is that it is being propounded in some
quarters as the proper substitute for Restoration.

The latter demands some knowledge and skill; the former is going to give unlimited
scope to those who will do the minimum to keep things going, but adding nothing to
enable them to make artistic sense.'

Often his work was totally misunderstood, as in the 1956 *Architects' Journal* review of
his proposals for the enlargement of St Edmundsbury Cathedral: 'The Dykes Bower report
seems to take it as axiomatic that the Scott work can and should be sacrificed, the Wastell
must not. It is difficult to see any force for this argument except sentimentality or pedestrian
antiquarianism … Dykes Bower has no intention of keeping-in-keeping in his design. Its
cable-stitch tracery argues vigorously with the old – so much so that straight contemporary,
or even a glass box, would come as not more of a jolt to the eye.' Here Astragal seemed
totally unaware of the re-use of early Kempe glass as the basis for the tracery design or the
retention of the Scott chancel, roof, tracery and glass for re-use (sadly both rood and tracery
have now gone). And only too often similar hurtful criticism had to be suffered in silence.
Over his bed in his house in the Little Cloister at Westminster Abbey hung an embroidered
text: 'Thou wilt keep him in perfect peace whose mind is stayed on Thee.'

In November 1971 Dykes Bower delivered an address entitled 'The Importance of
Style' to a meeting of the Cambridge Ecclesiological Society at Jesus College and this
later appeared in print in the *Architect* in December 1973. In October 1974 an address
was given to the Art Workers Guild on 'Conservation – What it Should Mean'; these
two papers, together with a later paper, 'The Re-ordering of Churches' read before the
Ecclesiological Society in October 1983 should be studied by all engaged in the fields of
conservation and ecclesiastical architecture.

We mourn the loss of an architect who achieved greatness through the integrity of
his architectural philosophy, which was always the expression of a profound Christian
faith. Whether his work setting forth that philosophy in material form will stand the
test of time only future generations will know, but his insistence on harmony and self-
effacement suggests that it will.

Let him have the last word:

'The prime need of religious buildings is an unmistakable atmosphere of reverence.
The concomitant of that is beauty, which will lift people out of themselves and quicken
their response to what a church stands for and has to offer.'

ALAN ROME
CHURCHSCAPE, NO.14, 1995

Bibliography

By Stephen Dykes Bower

1928

'John Wood, 1704-1754', *No. 35*, March 1928, pp.24–9.

1929

'The Gothic Revival: A Study In The History Of Taste, Kenneth Clark', *No. 35*, Autumn 1929, pp.5–12 (reprinted in *Victorian Society Annual*, 1994, pp.57–60).

1930–1

Review of *Oxford as it was, now is, and never should be* by R. W. Fennell, *RIBA Journal*, v.38, 1930–31, 24 January, p.181.

'The College of the Vicars Choral, Hereford.' *RIBA Journal*, v.38, 1930–31, 20 June, pp.595–8.

Review of Royal Commission on Historic Monuments, *Herefordshire*, *RIBA Journal*, v.38, 1930–31, 19 September, p.729.

1932

Review of *The Chained Library* by B. H. Streeter, *RIBA Journal*, v.39, 1931–2, 9 January, p.185.

Review of *A History of Religious Architecture* by Ernest H. Short, *RIBA Journal*, v.39, 1931–2, 27 June, p.876.

Review of *The Great Church Towers of England* by Frank J. Allen, *RIBA Journal*, v.39, 1931–2, 9 July p.715.

1933

Review of *Real Architecture* by T. H. Lyon, *RIBA Journal*, v.40, 1932–3, 25 February, p.326.

Review of *The Custos and College of the Vicars Choral of the Choir of the Cathedral Church of St Peter, Exeter*, by the Revd J. F. Chanter, *RIBA Journal*, v.41, 1933–4, 24 March, p.535.

Review of *Further Thoughts on the English Altar* by J. N. Comper, *RIBA Journal*, v.41, 1933–4, 25 November, p.90.

1934

'Organs and Organ Cases', *RIBA Journal*, 11 August 1934, pp.945–65.

Review of *Herefordshire* (RCHM volume), *RIBA Journal*, 24 November 1934, p.133.

1935

'Durham Revisited', *Architect and Building News*, 11 January 1935, pp.57–8.

Review of *Architecture and Music* by Alexander Walton, *RIBA Journal*, 9 February 1935, p.453.

'The Lady Chapel, St Wilfrid's, Harrogate', *Architect and Building News*, 12 July 1935, pp.54–5.

'The Greek Revival' (review of *Robert Mills, architect of the Washington Monument, 1781–1855*), *Architectural Review*, vol.78, July–December 1935, pp.107–8.

Review of *Early Victorian England* edited by G. M. Young, *RIBA Journal*, v.40, 10 August 1935, p.1053.

1936

Review of *The Railway Age* by C B Andrews, *RIBA Journal*, v.45, 1937–8, 7 March, p.450.

'Bridges' (review of *Ancient Bridges of Wales and Western England* by E. Jervoise, *Architectural Review*, v.80, July–December 1936, pp.120–2.

'Tablets and Inscriptions in Churches', *The Church Assembly News*, vol.13, No.10, October 1936, pp.228–32.

Review of *English Church Screens* by Aymer Vallance, *RIBA Journal*, v.44, 1936–7, 21 November, p.95 (also reviewed by Stephen Dykes Bower in *Architectural Review*, vol.81, April 1937, pp.189–90).

1939

'Thoughts of an architect-churchwarden', *The Times*, 7 February 1939, lecture for Church Crafts League at St Martin-in-the-Fields.

Review of *Church Building in the Nineteenth Century* by B. F. L. Clarke, *RIBA Journal*, v.46, 1938–9, 20 February, p.403.

1943

The Aspect of Cambridge, address to annual meeting of the Cambridge Preservation Society, 1943, pamphlet printed by W. Heffer & Sons, 1944, from *Cambridge Review*, 15 January 1944.

1945

Chichester in the Future, address delivery by Stephen Dykes Bower, Chichester Civic Society, Tuesday 4 December 1945 (pamphlet).

1948

'Cathedrals Today', address given at the Summer Festival, 1947, in *Friends of Ely Cathedral, Fifth Annual Report*, April 1948, pp.10–18.

1956

'The Inspection of Churches Measure', *RIBA Journal*, April 1956, pp.226–7.

1966

'The Architecture' in Edward Carpenter, ed., *A House of Kings, The History of Westminster Abbey*, London, John Baker, 1966, pp.387–404.

1967

'Cosmati Work in the Abbey', *Westminster Abbey Occasional Paper*, Spring 1967, pp.10–14.

1969

'The Stones of the Abbey', *Westminster Abbey Occasional Paper*, No.23, December 1969, pp.3–7.

1973

'Stained Glass in the Abbey', *Westminster Abbey Occasional Paper*, No.29, January 1973, pp.27–33.
'The Importance of Style', *Architect*, December 1973, pp.54–7.

1979

'Sir Gilbert Scott and Chester Cathedral', Newsletter of the Friends of Chester Cathedral, Christmas 1979, pp.9–15.

1980

'Sir Gilbert Scott's Religious Architecture' in Roger Dixon, ed., *Sir Gilbert Scott and the Scott Dynasty*, South Bank Architectural Papers, Polytechnic of the South Bank, pp.25–8.

1985

'Reordering' in *The Reordering of Churches*, papers read at a meeting of The Ecclesiological Society on 22 October 1983, published by S. C. Humphrey for The Ecclesiological Society, 1985, pp.5–11.
Preface to Margaret Stavradi, *Master of Glass. Charles Eamer Kempe 1837-1907*, Hatfield, Hertfordshire, John Taylor Book Ventures, 1985, p.7.

1993

'Reflections on the Appearance of Churches', lecture at the DAC conference, 1992, *Churchscape*, 11, 1993, pp.3–8.

'In Memoriam' (a personal account of his life), *Perspectives*, 10, February 1995, p.16

About Stephen Dykes Bower

'A Tribute', *Westminster Abbey Occasional Paper*, No.30, June 1973, pp.5–7 (E.F.C[arpenter]).

'Building to last: interview with Stephen Dykes Bower, an architect who has worked for the last 40 years in undiluted Gothic', *Building Design*, 3 December 1976, p.10.

James Bentley, 'In the great tradition', *Architects' Journal*, 20 April 1983, pp.40–3.

Gavin Stamp, 'Stephen Dykes Bower', *Spectator*, 30 April 1983, p.32.

Jennifer Benjamin, 'Crafts Survival', *Building Design*, 31 August 1984, pp.18–19.

Gavin Stamp, 'The English Tradition – Outsiders: a profile of Stephen Dykes Bower, enemy of modern architecture', *Spectator*, 12 April 1986, pp.20–1.

Anthony Symondson, *S E Dykes Bower: A Birthday Celebration*, Quendon, 1994.

Anthony Symondson, 'Stephen Dykes Bower and Victorian Church Architecture', *Victorian Society Annual*, 1994, pp.50–6.

Gavin Stamp. 'Gothic Revival', *Apollo*, vol clxi, no.519, pp.94–5

Quendon Court, By order of the executors of the late Stephen Dykes Bower, the contents of Quendon Court … for sale by auction, Wednesday 22nd February 1995. G. E. Sworder & Sons, Bishop's Stortford.

Alan Powers, 'The new Gothic' *Perspectives* 10, February 1995, pp.42–5.

'Architect leaves a Gothic pile' (Andrew Brown), *Independent*, 14 February 1995.

Alan Powers 'True Principles', *Crafts*, No.138, January–February 1996, pp.22–5.

'Fund snubs "mad" builder whose Gothic vision no one can see', *Guardian*, 20 May 1996.

Alan Powers, 'English caution' *Spectator*, 14 September 1996, pp.50–1.

Obituaries

British Institute of Organ Studies Journal, 1995, p.166 (Jim Berrow).

Church Times, 18 November 1994 (Margaret Holness).

Churchscape, No.14, 1995, pp.5–7 (Alan Rome).

Daily Telegraph, 14 November 1994 (Gavin Stamp).

Independent, 14 November 1994, p.14 (Anthony Symondson).

New York Times, 16 November 1994.

Organbuilder, October 1995, pp.20–1 (Michael Gillingham).

The Times, 14 November 1994, p.21 (Sir James Richards).

Index

Page numbers in italics refer to illustrations

Picture Credits

The author and publisher have made every effort to contact copyright holders and will be happy to correct, in subsequent editions, any errors or omissions that are brought to their attention.

Architectural Association Archives
3, 4,

Dykes Bower archive (courtesy of the Trustees of the S. E. Dykes Bower Will Trust) All photos of drawings by Keith Collie.
2, 6 (left), 7 (both, right Sydney Pitcher), 9 (top Sydney Pitcher, bottom Edwin C. Peckham,), 10 (left, H. K. Fox, right Sydney Pitcher), 11 (Robert Chalmers), 12, 13 (both) 15, 16 (all), 18 (Percy Wynne), 19, 20 (right), 26, 28, 29 (Aero Research Ltd), 34 (right), 35, 39 (Bedford Lemere Ltd), 46 (P.A.- Reuter), 51 (John Mowlem Ltd), 55 (bottom), 64, 65, 66 (both), 67, 68, 69, 84 (top and bottom left, Sydney W. Newbery; bottom right, Goddard & Gibbs), 89, 103, 104, 105, 106, 107, 117, 118, 121, 124 (bottom right), 125 (right), 127 (bottom), 132, 134, 135, (both), 136, 138, 140, 146, 150 (both), 151 (both), 154, 156 (both), 164 (London Stone Co.),

Elain Harwood
ii, 120,

English Heritage (James O. Davies)
Cover, 6 (right), 20 (left) 24, 30, 31 (both),

33, 34 (left), 80, 82, 83, 86 (both), 87, 88 (both), 96 (both), 99, 108, 114, 115 (both), 122, 124 (top and bottom right), 125 (left), 126, 127 (top), 128 (both), 129, 142 (both), 143, 148,

English Heritage (Steve Cole)
vi, xiv, xviii, 14, 21, 22 (all), 60, 70, 71, 72 (both), 74, 90 (bottom), 92, 93, 101 (both), 100, 113, 130, 131, 139,

English Heritage (National Monuments Record)
62, 90 (top)

Gavin Stamp
Back cover,

Ioana Marinescu
77

Lancing College
94, 95,

Paul Barker
116

Westminster Abbey
36, 38, 41, 42, 44, 48, 49, 50, 53, 54, 55 (top)